Building Bridges Together

The Comprehensive Guide to Fostering, Maintaining, and Thriving in Healthy Relationships for Couples

Selena Maddox

Summary

Chapter 1: Foundations of Connection

In this ever-evolving and fast-paced world, the ability to form meaningful connections with others is more crucial than ever before. Whether it is in our personal relationships or professional endeavors, the power of connection can shape our lives and determine our success. This chapter aims to delve into the foundations of connection, exploring the intricacies of human interaction, and unraveling the secrets to fostering deep and authentic connections.

Understanding Human Connection

At its core, human connection is about establishing a genuine and empathetic relationship with another person. It goes beyond superficial social interactions and delves into the realm of shared understandings, emotions, and mutual respect. Connection opens the doors to collaboration, understanding, and support, enabling us to navigate life's challenges more effectively.

The Importance of Connection

Studies have consistently shown that people who cultivate strong connections with others tend to have higher levels of happiness and well-being. Connection provides us with a sense of belonging, strengthens our mental and emotional health, and enhances our overall quality of life. It acts as a buffer against stress, loneliness, and depression, creating an emotional safety net that we can rely on during difficult times.

Foundations of Connection

Building a foundation for meaningful connection requires a set of core principles and skills. Let us explore these essential elements that can lay the groundwork for fostering deep and authentic connections in every aspect of our lives.

1. Active Listening

One of the fundamental pillars of connection is active listening. It involves fully engaging with the person you are communicating with and giving them your undivided attention. Active listening requires being present in the moment, eliminating distractions, and genuinely seeking to understand the other person's thoughts, feelings, and perspectives. By focusing on the speaker, we express our respect, build trust, and foster an environment conducive to open and honest communication.

2. Empathy

Empathy serves as a bridge that connects individuals on a deeper level. It is the ability to understand and share the feelings and experiences of others. Empathy requires us to put ourselves in someone else's shoes, suspending judgment, and being fully present with their emotions. By showing empathy, we create a safe space for vulnerability, leading to stronger connections and a greater sense of understanding.

3. Emotional Intelligence

Emotional intelligence plays a vital role in forging meaningful connections. It involves recognizing, understanding, and managing our own emotions, as well as being attuned to the emotions of others. By cultivating emotional intelligence, we can respond effectively to emotional cues, navigate conflicts, and establish mutually beneficial relationships. This self-awareness and empathy enable us to connect with others on a deeper, more authentic level.

4. Authenticity

Authenticity is the key to building genuine connections. By embracing our true selves and being honest in our interactions, we invite others to do the same. Authentic connections are built on trust and reciprocity, where individuals feel safe to be vulnerable without fear of judgment or rejection. Authenticity displays integrity, builds rapport, and lays the foundation for lasting connections.

5. Shared Values and Interests

Finding common ground with others can help strengthen connections. Shared values and interests create a sense of belonging and unity, giving individuals a platform to engage and connect on a deeper level. Identifying and nurturing these shared aspects can lead to rich and fulfilling connections that stand the test of time.

6. Vulnerability

To foster deep connections, we need to be open and vulnerable. Vulnerability involves sharing our fears, dreams, and struggles with others, allowing them to see our true self. By being vulnerable, we create an opportunity for reciprocal trust, as it encourages others to open up and share their own vulnerabilities. This level of openness and honesty is essential to building connections that withstand the trials and tribulations of life.

Understanding Relationship Structures: Exploring the different types of relationships and their foundational structures

Throughout our lives, we engage in various relationships that shape our existence and contribute to our personal growth. Relationships come in many forms, ranging from friendships and romantic partnerships to familial connections and professional alliances. Each relationship has its unique dynamics and structures, influencing the way we interact with others and the role they play in our lives. In this chapter, we will delve into the different types of relationships and their foundational structures, aiming to gain a deeper understanding of the intricacies behind human connections.

Section 1: Foundations of Relationships

1.1 - The essence of relationships:

At their core, relationships are built on connection and the shared experience of life. They serve as the bridge that bonds individuals together, enabling emotional support, personal growth, and a sense of belonging. Relationships encompass a diverse range of human interactions, each characterized by its nature, purpose, and depth.

1.2 - Elements contributing to relationship structures:

Various elements contribute to the formation and shaping of relationship structures. Communication, trust, respect, and reciprocity are among the fundamental ingredients that foster healthy and thriving relationships. Understanding the significance of these elements helps us appreciate the complexities and dynamics inherent in different relationships.

Section 2: Exploring Different Types of Relationships

2.1 - Familial Relationships:

Familial relationships are often the first connections we have in life. They include ties with parents, siblings, and extended family members. These relationships are typically characterized by blood or legal ties, providing a sense of belonging and shared history. Familial relationships play significant roles in shaping our identities, values, and beliefs, and they often form the bedrock for future social connections.

2.1.1 - Parent-child relationship:

The parent-child relationship is an essential bond that brings both joy and responsibility. Parents are tasked with nurturing and providing guidance to their children, while children look to their parents for love, care, and support. This relationship evolves throughout one's life, transitioning from dependency to a more mutually supportive and respectful connection.

2.1.2 - Sibling relationship:

Sibling relationships have their unique dynamics, influenced by factors such as birth order, age gaps, and individual personalities. Siblings often share a deep bond, offering companionship, rivalry, and a lifelong connection that endures even in the face of disagreements or distance.

2.2 - Friendships:

Friendships are voluntary relationships formed based on mutual affection, shared interests, and companionship. This type of relationship is characterized by trust, loyalty, and support. Friends provide emotional sustenance, serve as confidants, and share experiences, making friendships vital for our social and emotional well-being.

2.3 - Romantic Relationships:

Romantic relationships, also known as partnerships or marriages, revolve around emotional and physical intimacy. These relationships are marked by shared love, commitment, and a desire for a life-long partnership. Romantic relationships can be complex, as they require open communication, compromise, and a deep understanding of one another's needs and boundaries.

2.4 - Professional Relationships:

Professional relationships are formed within the workplace, academia, or any context that involves collaboration or shared goals. These relationships are typically task-oriented and require effective communication, respect, and teamwork to thrive. Professional relationships can range from formal, such as employer-employee dynamics, to more informal connections among colleagues or mentors.

Section 3: Relationship Structures and Dynamics

3.1 - Power Structures:

Power structures exist in all relationships and shape the distribution of influence, decision-making, and authority. These structures can vary significantly based on the type of relationship or societal norms.

Recognizing power imbalances and fostering equality within relationships is crucial for maintaining healthy and mutually beneficial connections.

3.2 - Codependency and Autonomy:

Codependency refers to an unhealthy pattern of reliance, where one person excessively depends on another for their emotional, physical, or psychological needs. On the other hand, autonomy emphasizes individual independence and self-reliance. Striking a balance between interdependence and personal freedom is key to developing sustainable and positive relationship structures.

Section 4: Nurturing and Maintaining Healthy Relationships

4.1 - Effective Communication:

Communication lies at the heart of all successful relationships. Expressing oneself authentically, actively listening, and resolving conflicts constructively are essential skills for fostering healthy connections. Understanding one another's communication styles and needs helps create an open and respectful relationship environment.

4.2 - Trust and Respect:

Building trust and respect is vital for any relationship to thrive. Trust is developed over time through consistent reliability, honesty, and integrity. Respect entails valuing each other's opinions, boundaries, and individuality. Nurturing these qualities strengthens the foundation of relationships and enhances their longevity.

4.3 - Cultivating Empathy and Emotional Intelligence:

Empathy and emotional intelligence play a crucial role in understanding and responding to the emotions and needs of others. Developing these skills helps create an environment of compassion, empathy, and support within relationships, leading to deeper connections and mutual growth.

Understanding the foundational structures and dynamics of different types of relationships equips us with the knowledge and tools necessary to navigate the complexities of human connections. By fostering effective communication, trust, and respect, we can cultivate and maintain healthy relationships that enrich our lives and contribute positively to the world around us. In the upcoming chapters, we will explore further aspects of relationship-building, including conflict resolution, maintaining intimacy, and creating healthy boundaries.

The Importance of Communication: Delving into why communication is the cornerstone of every healthy relationship

In the realm of human connection, relationships lie at the heart of what it means to exist and thrive. Each relationship we build, whether with a partner, friend, or family member, contributes to our personal growth and happiness. And at the core of every fruitful relationship lies effective communication. In this chapter, we will explore the significance of communication as the cornerstone of every healthy relationship. We will journey through the intricacies of communication, its types, barriers, and the transformative impact it can have on our connections with others.

The Essence of Communication

Communication is the lifeblood that nourishes relationships, providing a path for understanding and connection. It entails the exchange of information, thoughts, and emotions between individuals, enabling them to share their inner worlds and forge deeper bonds. Without communication, relationships become stagnant, leaving partners, friends, or family members feeling isolated and misunderstood.

Types of Communication

Communication takes various forms, including verbal, non-verbal, and written methods. Verbal communication, the most common form, involves spoken words and encompasses both face-to-face conversations and technology-driven exchanges. It allows for immediate response and offers the benefit of tone and intonation, ensuring clarity and minimizing misunderstandings.

Non-verbal communication, on the other hand, relies on body language, facial expressions, gestures, and other non-verbal cues. It provides essential context in conversations, often revealing hidden emotions or intentions. From a simple smile to a frown or raised eyebrow, non-verbal communication can convey messages that words sometimes struggle to articulate.

Written communication, such as texts, emails, or letters, bridges gaps created by distance or time constraints. While lacking the immediate feedback of verbal exchanges, it allows individuals to express themselves effectively, providing a lasting record that can be revisited, analyzed, and understood at one's own pace.

The Power of Listening

One vital aspect of communication often overlooked is the act of listening. Genuine listening is an active process of absorbing and comprehending what another person is communicating. It requires undivided attention, empathy, and a willingness to suspend our own judgments or preconceived notions.

Through active listening, we not only hear the words someone speaks but also try to understand the emotions and intentions underlying their message. This empathetic approach fosters trust and respect in relationships, making the speaker feel heard and valued. Furthermore, it paves the way for deeper connections that go beyond superficial exchanges.

Barriers to Effective Communication

While communication holds immense potential, numerous barriers can impede its effectiveness. These barriers may arise from external factors such as noise or distractions, but more often, they result from internal factors originating within individuals themselves.

One common barrier is the tendency to make assumptions or jump to conclusions before fully understanding a message. Prejudices, biases, and personal experiences can cloud our interpretation, hindering meaningful communication. Active awareness of these biases, coupled with an open mind, is key to breaking through these barriers and fostering genuine understanding.

Fear of judgment, rejection, or conflict can also hinder effective communication. When individuals feel unable to express their true thoughts or emotions due to these fears, misunderstandings and resentment can fester. Creating a safe and non-judgmental environment encourages open communication, allowing individuals to voice their concerns, needs, and desires freely.

The Transformative Impact of Communication

When communication thrives within a relationship, transformative outcomes can emerge. Firstly, effective communication builds trust. When individuals communicate openly and honestly, trust develops naturally, fostering authenticity and vulnerability. This trust forms a solid foundation that withstands the tests and trials that relationships often encounter.

Additionally, communication strengthens emotional bonds. The act of sharing one's experiences, both positive and negative, promotes emotional intimacy by fostering empathy, understanding, and support. Honest and open conversations allow partners, friends, or family members to truly connect, validating each other's emotions and strengthening their bond.

Moreover, communication in healthy relationships promotes growth and personal development. By openly exchanging ideas, values, and aspirations, individuals can learn from each other's unique perspectives. These conversations enable personal growth and broaden horizons, fostering an environment of constant self-improvement, both individually and collectively.

Effective communication is a deeply nuanced and essential aspect of developing and nurturing healthy relationships. Through verbal and non-verbal communication, active listening, and overcoming barriers, individuals can forge deep connections, build trust, and foster personal growth. Appreciating the significance of communication and investing time and effort into honing this skill can make all the difference in cultivating meaningful and lasting relationships. So, in our journey to unlock genuine connection and happiness, let us remember that communication is the cornerstone upon which we build our relationships, and it is through communication that we can thrive together.

Trust as the Keystone: Breaking down the pivotal role trust plays in building lasting connections

In the realm of human interactions, trust acts as a sacred glue that binds relationships and fosters deep connections. Trust is the cornerstone upon which friendships, romantic partnerships, and business alliances thrive. Without trust, these connections crumble and wither away, leaving behind a void of emptiness and broken bonds. Trust is not merely a fragile string that holds people together; rather, it is a robust keystone that withstands the test of time, fortifying relationships with its unwavering strength. In this chapter, we delve deeper into the multifaceted nature of trust, exploring its origin, elements, and the immense impact it has on building lasting connections.

The Genesis of Trust:

Trust, like a tiny seed, is planted in the soil of human connection. Its inception lies in the vulnerability of one person placing their faith in another. The genesis of trust can be traced back to the raw emotions of empathy and compassion. When one person shows genuine care and concern for another, a glimmer of trust begins to take root.

Empathy forms the bedrock of trust, enabling individuals to put themselves in someone else's shoes and comprehend their feelings and experiences. This understanding paves the way for compassion, which further nurtures trust and encourages individuals to extend a helping hand.

The Building Blocks of Trust:

Trust does not exist in isolation but is composed of several fundamental building blocks. These blocks intertwine, forming a sturdy foundation upon which trust can flourish. Authenticity, reliability, and consistency are three crucial elements that constitute the essence of trust.

Authenticity:

Authenticity is the true reflection of one's character, values, and intentions. It embodies the alignment between one's words and actions, allowing others to perceive their genuineness. When individuals express their true selves, they create an environment that fosters trust as it eliminates doubts and suspicions. Authenticity enables people to forge deeper connections, as it cultivates an atmosphere of openness and transparency.

Reliability:

Reliability is another pillar of trust. It is built on the foundation of fulfilling commitments and promises. Being reliable means that one can be counted on, consistently delivering on their word. When individuals exhibit reliability, it breeds a sense of dependability, assuring others that they can be trusted to do what they say they will. Reliability instills confidence, affirms trust, and strengthens relationships by demonstrating that one's actions align with their spoken commitments.

Consistency:

Consistency acts as a crucial element in building trust. It entails exhibiting a predictable pattern of behavior, manifesting a harmonious blend of authenticity and reliability. Consistency is the bridge between intentions and actions. When individuals display consistent behavior, it mollifies uncertainties and reinforces trust. Consistency builds a sense of security and stability, cementing connections by establishing a solid framework of trustworthiness.

The Power of Trust in Building Connections:

Trust exists on a spectrum that ranges from fragile to unbreakable. Fragile trust is akin to a delicate glass sculpture, easily shattered with a single blow. On the other end of the spectrum lies unbreakable trust, like a diamond, resilient and enduring. The strength of trust dictates the depth and longevity of connections. In friendships, trust becomes the cornerstone that supports vulnerability and emotional intimacy. Friends confide in each other, sharing their deepest fears, dreams, and secrets, knowing they can rely on the unwavering trust they have built. Trust allows friends to create a safe space where they can be their authentic selves, without the fear of being judged or rejected. This bond of trust fosters mutual respect, loyalty, and support, providing solace during tumultuous times and celebrating each other's triumphs.

In romantic relationships, trust serves as a binding force that weaves together the hearts of two individuals. It enables couples to be vulnerable, enabling a deep understanding and acceptance of each other's flaws and insecurities. Trust forms the bedrock of emotional intimacy, creating a space where partners can freely express themselves without fear of betrayal. Trust promotes harmony, respect, and open communication, allowing couples to weather the storms of life together, hand in hand.

In the realm of business, trust is the key that unlocks the door to successful collaborations and partnerships. It is the currency that fuels transactions and negotiations. Trust between business partners engenders confidence, ensuring that each party will act in the interest of the collective goal. Moreover, trust builds reputations and enhances credibility, attracting like-minded individuals and fostering fruitful collaborations. The pivotal role of trust fosters loyalty, integrity, and a sense of shared purpose, all of which are vital for long-term success in the business world.

Trust transcends societal boundaries and cultural differences. It is a universal language that resonates with every individual, regardless of their background or experiences. Trust acts as the fundamental building block upon which connections are fortified. Authenticity, reliability, and consistency form the bedrock of trust, forging unbreakable bonds and cultivating lasting relationships. Whether in friendships, romantic partnerships, or business alliances, trust is the lifeblood that nourishes connections, giving them meaning and purpose. It is through trust that individuals find solace, love, and success, creating a world filled with profound relationships and enduring connections.

Embracing Vulnerability: The benefits and necessities of being open and vulnerable in intimate relationships

In the realm of intimate relationships, vulnerability often gets misunderstood and underestimated. Many people associate vulnerability with weakness or fear, but in reality, being open and vulnerable in a relationship can lead to immense growth, trust, and deeper connections. In this chapter, we will explore the benefits and necessities of embracing vulnerability within intimate relationships. We will shine a light on the misconceptions surrounding vulnerability and uncover why vulnerability is an essential ingredient for creating fulfilling and lasting partnerships.

Unmasking Vulnerability:

To truly understand the concept of vulnerability, we must first dispel the myths that surround it. Many individuals mistakenly equate vulnerability with helplessness or a lack of strength. However, vulnerability is not about being weak, but rather about being courageous enough to reveal our authentic selves without any masks or barriers. It is about embracing our imperfections and insecurities and allowing our emotions to be seen and felt by others. Vulnerability is a fundamental human experience that brings us closer to each other, fostering empathy, and deepening connections.

Building Trust and Intimacy:

In any relationship, trust is the cornerstone that allows two people to bond and grow together. Vulnerability serves as the bridge to build that trust organically. When we show vulnerability by sharing our deepest thoughts, fears, and desires, we invite our partner into the most intimate parts of our being. By exposing our vulnerable side, we communicate that we trust our partner enough to share our authentic selves, creating a safe space where both individuals can open up without fear of judgment.

Through vulnerability, we also encourage reciprocity, enabling our partner to feel comfortable reciprocating in kind. The mutual exchange of vulnerability is a powerful catalyst for deepening intimacy, as it creates an atmosphere of emotional safety where both parties can explore their innermost thoughts and feelings together.

Encouraging Emotional Expression:

In many societies, emotional expression is often seen as a sign of weakness, particularly for men. However, by embracing vulnerability, we challenge this societal norm, allowing for the free and honest expression of emotions within our relationships. When we allow ourselves to be vulnerable, we give ourselves permission to experience and communicate our emotions genuinely. By doing so, we create an environment where both partners feel safe to express their emotions without fear of judgment or rejection.

Additionally, vulnerability fosters empathy and understanding between partners. When we open up and share our own vulnerabilities, we provide our partner with a glimpse into our world, allowing them to empathize and connect on a deeper level. This shared emotional experience enhances both partners' ability to support and console each other during challenging times, thus strengthening the bond between them.

Fostering Growth and Personal Development:
Intimate relationships provide a unique opportunity for personal growth and self-discovery. By embracing vulnerability, we allow ourselves to confront our deepest fears and insecurities, encouraging personal development. When we show vulnerability, we open ourselves up to feedback, constructive criticism, and new perspectives. This openness allows us to challenge our existing beliefs and attitudes, facilitating personal growth and transformation in the process.

Additionally, vulnerability within a relationship allows us to confront and heal past emotional wounds that often hinder our personal growth. Through open and raw communication, intimate partners can support each other in overcoming emotional traumas or fears, fostering healing and personal development.

In this chapter, we have explored the power of vulnerability in intimate relationships. We have debunked the myths surrounding vulnerability, highlighting its true nature as an act of courage rather than weakness. By embracing vulnerability, we can build trust, deepen intimacy, encourage emotional expression, and foster personal growth within our partnerships.

It is crucial to understand that vulnerability is a two-way street. To truly reap the benefits it brings, both partners must be willing to be open, honest, and emotionally available. Only then can vulnerability become the foundation upon which a fulfilling and lasting relationship is built.

Chapter 2: The Pillars of a Healthy Relationship

In the journey of life, relationships play a pivotal role in shaping our overall happiness and well-being. Whether it's a romantic partnership, a close friendship, or a family bond, healthy relationships form the foundation of our emotional, mental, and sometimes even physical health. Just like any structure, a healthy relationship requires a strong foundation in order to stand the test of time. In this chapter, we will explore the key pillars that contribute to a healthy relationship, providing you with valuable insights and guidance to nurture and strengthen these important connections.

Building Trust

Trust is the cornerstone of any successful relationship. Without trust, a relationship is inherently unstable and prone to be fragile. Trust is not something that can be demanded; it must be earned through consistent actions and words. It involves being reliable, keeping promises, and demonstrating integrity. In a healthy relationship, both partners must be able to rely on each other's honesty, loyalty, and support.

To build trust, effective communication is vital. Open, honest, and transparent conversations foster understanding and establish a sense of reliability. Listening attentively and empathetically to your partner's concerns and needs helps create a safe space for them to open up without fear of judgment. Trust is also nurtured through actions; following through on commitments and being dependable strengthens the foundation of trust in a relationship.

Respect and Equality

Respect and equality act as cornerstones for building a healthy relationship. Without mutual respect, resentment and dissatisfaction can cultivate, leading to an unhappy connection. Each partner should value the other's opinion, personal boundaries, and individuality. It's essential to recognize that everyone has the right to their own thoughts, feelings, and desires.

In a healthy relationship, both partners share the power and decision-making equally. Avoiding a power imbalance is crucial to fostering a sense of partnership in which both individuals have a voice and influence. Celebrating each other's successes, providing emotional support during challenging times, and encouraging personal growth are all manifestations of respect and equality within a relationship.

Effective Communication

Communication is the lifeblood of any relationship. It serves as the main channel through which partners express their needs, wants, and feelings. Effective communication involves both talking and listening. Verbal and non-verbal cues should be attentively observed to truly understand and connect with one another.

To improve communication in a relationship, active listening is essential. This involves giving your partner your full attention, avoiding interruptions, and making an effort to understand their perspective. Non-judgmental and non-defensive listening facilitates open dialogue and mutual understanding. Additionally, maintaining the habit of expressing appreciation and gratitude creates a positive communication dynamic, fostering a strong connection between partners.

Quality Time and Shared Experiences

Spending quality time together and creating shared experiences is a vital aspect of maintaining a healthy relationship. Engaging in activities that both partners enjoy strengthens the emotional bond and provides opportunities for laughter, learning, and growth. It's crucial to prioritize quality time regularly, despite busy schedules or other commitments.

When investing time in a relationship, being fully present is key. Minimize distractions, such as phones or work, and focus on engaging with your partner. This demonstrates their significance and reinforces the special connection you share. Whether it's a romantic date night, a weekend getaway, or simply cooking a meal together, these shared experiences create precious memories and deepen the relationship.

Teamwork and Support

In a healthy relationship, partners function as a team, supporting and encouraging each other through life's ups and downs. Building a strong support system fosters a sense of security and shows that no matter the circumstances, you have each other's back.

Supporting your partner can take many forms, including actively listening to their concerns, offering advice when requested, and providing comfort during difficult times. Sharing responsibilities, whether it's household chores or decision-making, helps distribute the load and fosters a sense of equality within the relationship. Remember, a strong team built on trust and support can conquer any obstacle that comes their way.

Conflict Resolution

Conflict is an inevitable part of any relationship. However, how conflicts are approached and resolved can make or break the health of a connection. Healthy relationships are not devoid of disagreements but rather characterized by effective conflict resolution strategies.

In resolving conflicts, it's important to nurture a collaborative atmosphere rather than an adversarial one. Practicing active listening, avoiding blame and criticism, and using "I" statements instead of accusatory language are key components of resolving conflicts constructively. Compromise and finding win-win solutions demonstrates the willingness of both partners to put the relationship's well-being above individual desires. Ultimately, approaching conflicts as opportunities for growth and understanding can foster a deeper connection and strengthen the relationship.

Building and maintaining a healthy relationship requires commitment, effort, and a solid foundation. By incorporating the pillars outlined in this chapter – trust, respect and equality, effective communication, quality time and shared experiences, teamwork and support, and conflict resolution – you can create a strong and fulfilling bond. Remember, relationships are living entities that deserve continuous nurturing and care. By prioritizing these pillars, you will build a resilient and harmonious relationship that stands the test of time.

Emotional Availability: Recognizing and promoting emotional presence in relationships

In this chapter, we explore the concept of emotional availability and its significance in fostering healthy and fulfilling relationships. Emotional availability refers to an individual's capacity to be fully present and receptive to the emotional needs of their partners. It involves recognizing, validating, and responding to one another's emotional cues with empathy and understanding. Developing emotional availability is crucial in forming deep connections and maintaining long-lasting relationships.

Understanding Emotional Availability

Emotional availability encompasses a range of behaviors and attitudes necessary for establishing and maintaining healthy emotional connections. It involves being in touch with one's own emotions while also being attuned to the emotions of others. Emotional availability is rooted in self-awareness, empathy, and effective communication.

Self-Awareness

To be emotionally available to others, one must first be aware of their own emotions. Recognizing and accepting one's feelings allows for a deeper understanding of oneself, creating a solid foundation for emotional connection. Furthermore, self-awareness enables individuals to articulate their emotions and needs, enhancing open and honest communication within relationships.

Empathy

Empathy plays a crucial role in emotional availability as it involves the ability to understand and share another person's emotions. Cultivating empathy deepens our connection with our partners and fosters an environment of trust, compassion, and mutual understanding. By acknowledging and validating our partner's emotions, we create a safe space for them to express themselves fully.

Effective Communication

Clear and effective communication is fundamental to emotional availability. Sharing one's thoughts and feelings openly and honestly enables partners to better understand each other's emotional experiences. By actively listening to one another and responding with empathy, couples can avoid misunderstandings and build a genuine emotional connection.

Recognizing Emotional Availability

Recognizing emotional availability in oneself and others is essential for developing healthy relationships. The following signs may indicate emotional availability:

1. Mindful Listening: Emotionally available individuals actively listen to their partners, focusing on their needs, concerns, and emotions. They provide undivided attention, demonstrating that they genuinely care about their partner's experiences.

2. Empathetic Responses: Emotional availability manifests through empathetic responses to one another's emotions. Understanding and validating their partner's feelings and being supportive without judgment builds emotional rapport and strengthens the relationship bond.

3. Open Vulnerability: Emotionally available partners are willing to be vulnerable and share their own emotions and experiences. They create a safe space for their partners to do the same, fostering trust and emotional intimacy.

4. Emotional Consistency: Emotional availability includes consistent expressions of love, care, and support. Emotionally available

individuals are responsive to their partner's emotional needs and consistently provide reassurance and comfort.

Promoting Emotional Availability

Developing emotional availability requires effort and commitment from both partners. The following strategies can promote emotional presence and enhance emotional availability in relationships:

1. Cultivating Self-Awareness: Engaging in self-reflection allows individuals to better understand their own emotional responses and triggers. Practices such as journaling, meditation, and therapy can help develop self-awareness, fostering emotional availability.

2. Practicing Empathy: Empathy can be cultivated through active listening and perspective-taking. Seeking to understand and validate your partner's emotions helps create an environment of emotional safety and trust.

3. Encouraging Open Communication: Establishing open and honest lines of communication builds emotional availability. Encourage your partner to express their feelings and provide reassurance that their emotions will be acknowledged and validated.

4. Developing Emotional Intelligence: Emotional intelligence refers to the ability to recognize, understand, and manage emotions.

Developing emotional intelligence allows for better emotional regulation, empathy, and communication within relationships.

5. Making Time for Emotional Connection: Prioritizing quality time together and engaging in activities that foster emotional connection strengthens the emotional bond between partners. Shared experiences, such as date nights or weekend getaways, allow for deeper emotional intimacy.

Emotional availability is a cornerstone of healthy and fulfilling relationships. By recognizing the significance of emotional presence, individuals can cultivate greater empathy, establish open channels of communication, and develop emotional intimacy with their partners. The journey towards emotional availability begins with self-awareness and is nurtured by consistent effort and mindfulness. By fostering emotional availability, couples can create lasting and meaningful connections, enriching their relationship experiences.

Bridging Relationship Expectations: Understanding and aligning shared goals and dreams

In every relationship, whether it be romantic, familial, or even between friends, shared goals and dreams play a pivotal role in its success and longevity. The ability to understand and align these expectations is crucial for a healthy and fulfilling connection. In this chapter, we will explore the significance of bridging relationship expectations, delving into the importance of communication, compromise, and mutual understanding. By developing a deep comprehension of one another's aspirations, a strong foundation can be built, nurturing a relationship that withstands the test of time.

The Power of Communication:

Effective communication serves as the cornerstone of any successful relationship. To bridge relationship expectations, partners must engage in open and honest conversations, sharing their desires and dreams with one another. By genuinely listening and expressing themselves, individuals can gain insight into each other's values, ambitions, and aspirations.

Furthermore, communication builds trust and understanding, fostering a sense of inclusivity within the relationship. In a safe and non-judgmental space, partners can voice their hopes, fears, and objectives and, in doing so, create a strong emotional connection.

Compromise: The Art of Balancing Individual Goals:

While shared goals and dreams are essential, it is equally crucial to recognize and respect each individual's aspirations. Relationships thrive when partners strike a balance between aligning their expectations and allowing space for personal growth and fulfillment. To bridge relationship expectations successfully, compromise becomes an art form.

Compromise involves a willingness to find common ground and make sacrifices. Each partner must be open to adapting their individual expectations to accommodate the shared vision for the future. Through compromise, a couple can navigate the delicate balance between honoring individual dreams and fostering the growth of the relationship as a whole.

Understanding and Empathy:

To bridge relationship expectations effectively, it is vital to cultivate empathy and develop a profound understanding of your partner's goals and dreams. This requires delving deeper, beyond surface-level conversations, and truly grasping the underlying motivations and desires.

Empathy involves putting oneself in the shoes of the other person and looking at life through their perspective. It allows for a genuine appreciation of their goals, dreams, and the emotions attached to them. By seeking this understanding, individuals can strengthen their emotional connection and develop greater appreciation and support for one another.

The Role of Shared Experiences:

Shared experiences play a pivotal role in bridging relationship expectations. Engaging in activities together that align with both partners' aspirations establishes a sense of unity and allows for shared growth. These experiences can be small or significant, ranging from adventure trips to pursuing a new hobby together.

Sharing experiences creates memories and strengthens the emotional bond within the relationship. Additionally, it provides an opportunity for partners to witness and support each other's aspirations firsthand, fostering a deeper understanding and appreciation for one another's dreams.

Navigating Differences:

In any relationship, differences are inevitable. Each partner brings their unique backgrounds, experiences, and perspectives, which can lead to differing expectations and dreams. However, navigating these differences is crucial to bridging relationship expectations successfully.

Rather than viewing differences as obstacles or sources of conflict, they can be seen as opportunities for growth and learning. Embracing diversity within a relationship allows partners to expand their horizons, challenge their own beliefs, and foster a mutually beneficial environment. By valuing and respecting these differences, partners can bridge the gap between their expectations and explore new possibilities together.

Continual Growth and Evolution:

Relationships are not static; they require continual growth and evolution. Bridging relationship expectations is an ongoing process that requires regular check-ins and re-evaluations. As individuals evolve, so do their dreams and desires. To ensure alignment, partners must maintain open lines of communication and regularly discuss their goals.

Creating a shared vision for the future requires adaptability and the willingness to grow alongside one another. By embracing change and being open to redefining expectations, partners can nurture a relationship that remains dynamic and flourishing.

Bridging relationship expectations is an intricate yet essential process that lays the foundation for a successful and fulfilling connection. Through effective communication, compromise, understanding, shared experiences, and navigating differences, partners can align their dreams and goals, fostering a relationship that grows and evolves together.

By nurturing this bridge, individuals can achieve a deeper emotional connection and build a future that encompasses their shared aspirations. May this chapter serve as a guiding light on this journey, empowering individuals to bridge their relationship expectations and forge stronger, more resilient connections.

Keeping the Spark Alive: Strategies for maintaining passion and intimacy over time

When we first fall in love, everything seems magical. Our hearts race, our palms sweat, and we feel an undeniable connection with our partner. It's as though we are floating on cloud nine, and nothing could ever diminish the intensity of our feelings. However, as time passes, relationships often lose some of their initial spark. This doesn't mean that love has faded; it simply means that the initial passion has evolved into something deeper and more meaningful. In this chapter, we will explore strategies for maintaining passion and intimacy over time, helping you create a fulfilling and lasting relationship.

Building Emotional Intimacy:

1. Effective Communication: Communication is the foundation of any successful relationship. As we spend more time with someone, it's essential to communicate our thoughts, needs, and desires openly. Encourage and practice active listening, making your partner feel heard and understood. Creating an environment of trust and open conversation will strengthen the emotional bond between you and

your loved one.

2. Show Empathy and Compassion: Make an effort to understand your partner's perspective and validate their emotions. Even if you don't agree with them, showing empathy and compassion can create a safe space for open dialogue and strengthen emotional intimacy.

3. Quality Time: In our fast-paced world, it's crucial to set aside quality time for one another. Whether it's a weekly date night or simply a quiet evening together, undivided attention helps foster emotional connection and keeps the spark alive.

4. Respect Each Other's Individuality: As a relationship progresses, it's essential to respect each other's unique needs, interests, and personal space. Encourage personal growth and individual pursuits, allowing each partner to maintain their individuality while still nurturing the couple's bond.

Nurturing Physical Intimacy:

1. Prioritize Sexual Intimacy: Physical intimacy is a vital component of a healthy relationship. Keep the passion alive by prioritizing your sexual connection with your partner. Explore each other's desires, try new things, and make an effort to deepen your physical bond through affection and sexual exploration.

2. Invest in Touch: Physical touch is an integral part of any intimate relationship. Hugs, cuddles, and gentle caresses throughout the day can strengthen your emotional connection and reignite the spark between you. Don't underestimate the power of touch; it can speak volumes when words fall short.

3. Frequent Non-sexual Intimacy: Physical intimacy isn't solely about sex. It's equally important to engage in non-sexual physical intimacy, such as holding hands, giving massages, or simply snuggling on the couch. These acts can bring you closer together and create an intimate atmosphere outside of the bedroom.

4. Practice Open Communication about Sexual Desires: Don't shy away from discussing your sexual desires and fantasies with your partner. Honest and open conversations about your needs and expectations can help maintain passion and prevent any potential disconnect.

Keeping the Flame Alive:

1. Continual Self-Reflection: To keep the spark alive, it's important to engage in self-reflection regularly. Ensure that you are taking care of your own emotional and physical well-being. By loving and respecting yourself, you can bring your best self to the relationship and ignite passion within your partner.

2. Surprise and Excite: Surprise your partner occasionally with gestures of love and appreciation. Plan a romantic weekend getaway, leave sweet notes, or cook their favorite meal. Small surprises and acts of thoughtfulness can go a long way in rejuvenating the relationship and maintaining excitement.

3. Share New Experiences: Trying new activities together can reignite the passion and excitement within a relationship. Sign up for a dance class, plan a hiking trip, or simply explore a new hobby together. Shared experiences create lasting memories and provide opportunities for growth both as individuals and as a couple.
4. Celebrate Each Other: Take the time to celebrate your partner's accomplishments and milestones. Celebrations don't need to be extravagant; it can be as simple as acknowledging their hard work or surprising them with a small gift. Expressing pride and admiration for their achievements reinforces love and respect in the relationship.
Maintaining the spark and intimacy in a long-term relationship is a continuous effort that requires commitment, understanding, and open communication. By building emotional intimacy, nurturing physical connection, and keeping the flame alive through self-reflection and shared experiences, couples can create a relationship that is both passionate and fulfilling. Remember, the evolution of love is a beautiful journey, and by investing in each other, you can deepen your bond and create a love that lasts a lifetime.

The Role of Independence: How to balance togetherness with individual growth

As human beings, we are inherently social creatures. Our desire for connection and belonging is deeply ingrained within us. We thrive in communities where we can share our experiences, emotions, and ideas with others. However, amidst the warmth of togetherness, it is equally crucial to nurture our individual selves. This delicate balancing act between togetherness and independence is the focus of this chapter. We will explore the significance of independence in fostering personal growth and how it can harmoniously coexist with the bonds of togetherness.

Embracing Independence for Personal Growth:
Independence plays a fundamental role in our personal growth and development. It empowers us to explore new horizons, discover our passions, and cultivate a sense of self-worth. When we become overly reliant on others for validation, decision-making, or emotional support, we limit our potential for growth. Independence liberates us from the shackles of conformity, allowing us to shape our own path and forge our unique identities.

Contrary to popular belief, independence does not equate to detachment or isolation. Instead, it provides a solid foundation for us to weave the threads of our individuality into the fabric of togetherness. By asserting our independence, we can contribute more meaningfully to our relationships, communities, and society as a whole. When we continuously pursue personal growth, we bring fresh perspectives, innovative ideas, and a renewed sense of purpose to the collective tapestry of humanity.

Balancing Togetherness and Independence:
Finding the delicate balance between togetherness and independence is an art form that requires conscious effort and self-reflection. It is essential to navigate this terrain with grace, both for the sake of our own growth and the harmony of our relationships. Let us explore some key strategies for striking this balance:

1. Self-Awareness:
Developing self-awareness is crucial when seeking the right balance between togetherness and independence. It involves understanding our needs, values, strengths, and weaknesses. By gaining insight into who we are as individuals, we can align our actions and decisions with our authentic selves. This self-awareness not only helps us in personal growth but also enables us to establish healthier and more fulfilling connections with others.

2. Communication:

Open and honest communication holds the key to maintaining harmony between togetherness and independence. We must articulate our desires, aspirations, and boundaries to others while encouraging them to do the same. Creating an environment that promotes dialogue and active listening enables meaningful connections without compromising personal growth. Through effective communication, we can establish mutual respect, understanding, and support for one another's independent journeys.

3. Setting Boundaries:

Boundaries act as a protective shield for our personal growth while ensuring the preservation of our relationships. As individuals, we must define our limits and communicate them to those around us. Healthy boundaries prevent us from becoming overwhelmed or losing ourselves in the needs and expectations of others. Embracing boundaries cultivates a healthy sense of independence while fostering mutual respect and understanding within our interconnected web of relationships.

4. Cultivating Interdependence:

Interdependence is the sweet spot between excessive dependence and complete independence. It embraces the idea that while we are separate individuals, we are also interconnected with one another. When we cultivate interdependence, we create symbiotic relationships that encourage personal growth and allow us to thrive collectively. This mindset acknowledges that we can rely on others for support, guidance, and collaboration, without compromising our individual identities or potential for growth.

5. Time for Reflection:

Amidst the constant hustle and bustle of our lives, it is essential to carve out time for self-reflection. Reflection helps us assess the balance between togetherness and independence. It allows us to introspect, evaluate our choices, and make necessary adjustments. Regular reflection nurtures our growth by helping us identify areas where we may be stifled by excessive togetherness or neglecting our independent pursuits. It serves as a compass to guide us back to equilibrium.

In this chapter, we dove into the profound role of independence in our personal growth and explored how it can be balanced with togetherness. Independence is not a threat to our connections but rather an essential ingredient to foster genuine relationships grounded in mutual respect and understanding. By nurturing our individual growth, we bring unique gifts to the table of togetherness, enhancing the richness of our collective experiences. May this exploration inspire you to embrace the journey towards balance, recognizing that our independent growth can coexist harmoniously with the interconnected tapestry of human connection.

Chapter 3: Overcoming Relationship Roadblocks

Relationships are beautiful and fulfilling aspects of our lives, but they can also present us with numerous challenges and roadblocks. From miscommunication to trust issues, we consistently face hurdles that threaten to break the bond we have formed with our loved ones. However, it is crucial to remember that these roadblocks are not insurmountable and can be effectively overcome with the right mindset and approach. In this chapter, we will explore various strategies and tools to navigate through the most common relationship roadblocks and build stronger, healthier connections.

1. Communication Breakdown: The Foundation of All Issues

Communication is the cornerstone of any successful relationship. When we fail to communicate effectively, misunderstandings arise, emotions get bottled up, and resentment starts to grow. To overcome this roadblock, we must first acknowledge its significance and commit to improving our communication skills.

One essential aspect of effective communication is active listening. Truly hearing and understanding our partner's perspective fosters empathy and helps bridge the gap between two different viewpoints. By actively listening, we demonstrate that we value their thoughts and opinions, which enhances the overall communication experience.

Honesty is another fundamental element of healthy communication. It is essential to express our feelings openly and honestly, even if it means discussing difficult topics. Honesty lays the groundwork for trust and fosters an environment where both parties feel safe speaking their minds.

Furthermore, being aware of nonverbal communication cues like body language and facial expressions can help bridge potential communication gaps. These cues often reveal emotions that words alone may not express, leading to a deeper understanding of our partner's feelings.

2. The Trust Dilemma: Learning to Build and Rebuild Trust

Trust is the very foundation of any successful relationship. Without trust, doubts and insecurities start to creep in, gradually eroding the bond we share with our partner. Overcoming trust issues requires patience, understanding, and a willingness to cultivate trust anew.

Building trust initially involves consistency and reliability. By being true to our word and following through with our commitments, we demonstrate that we can be trusted. Similarly, small gestures of integrity and honesty, even when they seem inconsequential, contribute to building a solid foundation of trust.

Rebuilding trust in a relationship that has suffered a breach requires more effort. It is vital to address the underlying issues and take responsibility for any actions that have caused harm. Open and transparent communication, accompanied by sincere apologies and a genuine desire to change, can begin to mend the broken trust.

Rebuilding trust also involves allowing time for healing. It is essential to recognize that trust is not restored overnight; it is a gradual process that requires patience and understanding.

3. Conflict Resolution: Navigating Contention with Grace

Conflict is a natural part of any relationship and, when handled appropriately, can foster growth and understanding. However, if conflicts are not resolved effectively, they can become relationship roadblocks and lead to resentment and distance. Understanding healthy conflict resolution is crucial for maintaining a harmonious partnership.

To overcome conflict roadblocks, it is important to approach disagreements with empathy and respect. By understanding our partner's perspective, we can find common ground and work toward a mutually beneficial solution.

Active listening and effective communication play pivotal roles in conflict resolution. It is vital to express our feelings and concerns without attacking or blaming our partner. Using "I" statements can help avoid accusatory language and keep the discussion focused on finding a solution.

Compromise is another key aspect of resolving conflicts. It involves finding middle ground and being willing to meet halfway. Compromise strengthens the relationship by showing a willingness to prioritize the needs and desires of both partners.

If necessary, seeking professional help, such as couple's therapy, can be incredibly beneficial in navigating complex conflicts. Therapists provide an unbiased perspective and guide couples through the resolution process, facilitating healing and growth.

4. Intimacy Challenges: Reigniting the Flame

Intimacy is an integral part of any romantic relationship, but it can sometimes be challenging to maintain it over the long term. Stress, lack of time, or even monotony can lead to a decline in intimacy. Overcoming these roadblocks requires effort, vulnerability, and a desire to reignite the flame.

One approach to reigniting intimacy is creating opportunities for quality time together. Setting aside dedicated time for activities that bring both partners joy and foster connection can help reignite the flame. Whether it is going on dates, engaging in shared hobbies, or simply having meaningful conversations, these moments contribute to a deeper bond.

Exploring new experiences together can be an exciting way to reignite passion and intimacy. Trying new activities, traveling to new places, or even stepping out of our comfort zones can help break the monotony and inject freshness into the relationship.

Effective communication about desires and needs is crucial when addressing intimacy. Sharing openly and honestly about what both partners find pleasurable and satisfying allows for a more fulfilling and intimate connection.

Finally, it is essential to remember that intimacy extends beyond the physical realm. Emotional intimacy, formed through vulnerability, trust, and authentic connection, is equally vital. Sharing fears, dreams, and concerns fosters a deeper connection and a sense of emotional fulfillment.

Overcoming relationship roadblocks is a continuous journey that requires effort, patience, and dedication from both partners. By focusing on effective communication, building and rebuilding trust, resolving conflicts with empathy, and nurturing intimacy, we can navigate the challenges that arise and build stronger, healthier relationships.

Remember, each relationship is unique, and there is no one-size-fits-all solution. The strategies and tools outlined in this chapter will serve as a starting point for your personal journey towards overcoming relationship roadblocks. Adapt them to your specific situation, and keep learning and growing together with your partner.

Bridge Over Troubled Water: Approaches for navigating conflicts and disagreements

Conflicts and disagreements are an inevitable part of our lives. Whether they occur in personal relationships, professional settings, or even within ourselves, conflicts can be challenging and emotionally charged. However, it is crucial to remember that conflicts also offer opportunities for growth, understanding, and strengthening relationships if they are approached with the right mindset and strategies.

In this chapter, we will explore various approaches for navigating conflicts and disagreements, aiming to provide you with practical tools to build bridges over troubled waters. By embracing these approaches, you will gain insights into effective communication, conflict resolution techniques, and the power of empathy and understanding.

Understanding Conflict:

To effectively navigate conflicts, it is essential to grasp their nature and underlying causes. Conflicts typically arise due to differences in needs, values, perspectives, or goals. They can manifest as a clash of ideas, opinions, or desires. Recognizing that conflicts are not inherently negative but merely a result of divergent views sets the foundation for finding mutual understanding and resolution.

Approach 1: Active Listening and Empathy:

One of the most powerful tools in navigating conflicts is active listening. When engaged in a disagreement, people often focus on expressing their own thoughts and feelings without truly listening to the other party. By actively listening, you demonstrate respect, validate the other person's perspective, and create space for authentic dialogue.

To practice active listening, begin by suspending judgment and resisting the urge to interrupt. Focus on the speaker's words, tone, and non-verbal cues to gain a deeper understanding of their emotions and underlying concerns. Reflecting back what you have understood, using statements such as "What I am hearing you say is..." or "It seems like you are feeling..." helps the speaker feel heard and acknowledged.

Additionally, practicing empathy is vital in conflict resolution. Empathy involves putting yourself in the other person's shoes, attempting to understand their experience, and validating their emotions. This does not mean you have to agree with them, but rather showing that you care and are willing to empathize can defuse tension and pave the way for finding common ground.

Approach 2: Effective Communication:

Conflict resolution heavily relies on clear and effective communication. Misunderstandings or poor communication often exacerbate conflicts, leading to further division. To communicate effectively during conflicts, it is crucial to practice assertiveness, active engagement, and mindful dialogue.

Assertiveness entails expressing your thoughts, feelings, and needs honestly and respectfully. It involves using "I" statements instead of accusatory language, promoting ownership and understanding. This approach encourages open communication and gives the other person the opportunity to respond without feeling attacked or defensive.

Active engagement during conflicts means actively involving oneself in the conversation, showing interest, and asking open-ended questions. This active participation demonstrates your commitment to resolution and helps uncover underlying issues. Mindful dialogue focuses on being present in the moment, avoiding distractions, and giving the conversation the attention it deserves. Mindfulness enhances understanding, minimizes miscommunication, and fosters a calmer and more productive atmosphere.

Approach 3: Collaborative Problem-Solving:

Collaboration is a powerful approach when navigating conflicts. It involves working together with the other party to find creative solutions that address each side's needs and concerns. Collaborative problem-solving requires an open mind, flexibility, and a willingness to consider alternative viewpoints.

Start by establishing a common goal that both parties can work towards. This shared objective helps shift the focus from the conflict itself to finding a solution that benefits everyone involved. Encourage brainstorming ideas and suggestions, valuing each person's contribution. By actively involving both parties in the decision-making process, you increase the chances of finding a mutually satisfactory resolution.

Approach 4: Mediation and Third-Party Involvement:

In some situations, conflicts may escalate or become particularly challenging to resolve without external support. This is where mediation and third-party involvement play a crucial role. Mediation involves the assistance of a neutral third party who facilitates communication and negotiation between the conflicting parties.

Mediators help diffuse tension, ensure fairness, and guide the conversation towards areas of compromise. Their role is to facilitate understanding, encourage active listening, and help generate options for resolution. A skilled mediator can navigate complex conflicts, offer new perspectives, and assist in finding common ground where both parties feel heard and satisfied.

Navigating conflicts and disagreements is undoubtedly a complex and sometimes overwhelming task. However, with the right approaches and a commitment to open communication, empathy, and collaboration, conflicts can be transformed into opportunities for growth and understanding.

By practicing active listening, effective communication, collaborative problem-solving, and seeking third-party mediation when necessary, you can build bridges over troubled waters and foster healthier, more harmonious relationships in all areas of your life.

The Challenge of Change: Adapting and evolving together amidst life's unpredictabilities

Life, as we all know it, is inherently dynamic and ever-changing. From the flux of seasons to the shifting tides of emotions, everything around us is in a constant state of transformation. The ability to adapt and evolve amidst life's unpredictabilities is a profound challenge that we all face. This chapter explores the intricacies of this challenge, delving into the essence of adaptation and evolution while illuminating the ways in which humanity can navigate this complex journey together.

The Path of Adaptation: Embracing the Winds of Change

Change is an integral part of life, shaping the world around us and influencing our individual paths. As humans, we often find ourselves grappling with the unknown, fearing the uncertain outcome of each transitional phase. However, to truly unlock the joys of existence, it is vital that we learn to embrace change wholeheartedly, for it is through adaptation that we discover our true potential.

Throughout history, civilizations have risen and fallen, often in response to their ability to adapt to ever-evolving circumstances. From ancient empires that perished due to stubbornness, to modern societies flourishing through adaptation, the lessons of those who came before us serve as guiding lights in our quest for survival. By observing the nature of change and willingly adapting to it, we can pave a path towards growth and fulfillment.

The Complexity of Adaptation: Navigating Choppy Waters

Adapting to change can be an arduous process, rife with challenges and unforeseen obstacles. Our resistance to leaving our comfort zones often stems from a fear of the unknown; we prefer the familiar, the predictable. However, this innate resistance can stifle our growth potential and hinder our abilities to navigate the complexities of life.

In order to successfully adapt, we must first acknowledge the fluidity of existence. We must recognize that change is not an external force working against us but an integral part of our human experience. By shifting our perspective and embracing change as an opportunity for growth, we open ourselves up to countless possibilities.

Moreover, adaptation is not an individual endeavor; it is a collective journey that requires empathy, resilience, and collaboration. As humans, we are social beings, interconnected and interdependent.

To smoothly navigate the tumultuous waters of change, we must come together, supporting, and uplifting one another.

Evolution: The Eternal Dance of Progress

Parallel to adaptation, evolution is the process through which species, societies, and ideas develop over time. It is an implacable force that pushes boundaries, molds identities, and shapes the course of history. Humanity, too, is subject to this eternal dance, constantly evolving to meet the demands and challenges of an ever-changing world.

The evolution of humanity can be witnessed in our collective advancements — from the discovery of fire to the advent of artificial intelligence. It is through evolution that we have triumphed over adversity, innovating and adapting to improve the human condition. As we stand on the precipice of the future, our ability to continue evolving will determine our success in the face of new challenges.

The Power of Unity: Thriving Together

In the face of daunting change, unity is our greatest strength. It is through shared experiences, collective efforts, and collaboration that we can navigate the labyrinth of life's unpredictabilities. By fostering a sense of togetherness, we can create a support system that uplifts us in times of triumph and steadies us during moments of uncertainty.

Unity also allows for diversity to flourish. Each individual brings a unique perspective, skill set, and background to the table. By embracing and harnessing these differences, we can amplify our collective abilities, unraveling the deepest mysteries of existence and finding novel solutions to complex problems.

Through unity, we cultivate resilience. We learn to bounce back from adversity, finding strength within ourselves and each other. Together, we can transform change from a daunting adversary into an exhilarating journey of growth and empowerment.

In the magnificent symphony of life, adaptation and evolution serve as the steppingstones towards a brighter, more prosperous future. Although change may seem intimidating and unpredictable, it is through resilience, collaboration, and collective consciousness that we can navigate these challenges. By embracing the winds of change, evolving in harmony, and committing to adaptability, we cultivate a society that thrives amidst life's unpredictabilities. Together, we unlock the infinite joys of existence, marching boldly towards a shared tomorrow.

Healing Relationship Ruptures: Techniques for repairing trust and reconnecting after betrayals

Human connections are intricate and delicate, capable of bringing immense joy and fulfillment, but also vulnerable to ruptures and betrayals that can shatter trust. Healing relationship ruptures requires tremendous effort, empathy, and a genuine desire to repair the damage caused. In this chapter, we will explore various techniques aimed at rebuilding trust and reconnecting after facing betrayals in our closest relationships. By implementing these techniques, individuals can strive towards healing the wounds of betrayal and fostering a healthier, stronger bond with their loved ones.

Understanding the Impact of Betrayal:

Betrayals can manifest in numerous ways, such as infidelity, broken promises, or breaches of confidentiality. Regardless of the specific form, betrayals inflict deep emotional wounds, paving the way for mistrust, resentment, and despair. Recognizing the immense impact betrayals can have on relationships is crucial for both parties involved. The person who betrayed must acknowledge the harm they have caused, while the betrayed must find a way to navigate through a whirlwind of emotions and decide if reconciliation is possible.

1. Honest Communication:

The foundation for healing relationship ruptures lies in open and honest communication. Both parties need to create a safe space to express their thoughts, emotions, and concerns. Opening up and engaging in vulnerable conversations can foster empathy and understanding from both sides. The person who caused the betrayal must genuinely express remorse, take responsibility for their actions, and be willing to listen without defensiveness. Equally important, the betrayed individual must be brave enough to articulate their pain, expectations, and doubts without suppressing their emotions.

2. Re-establishing Boundaries:

A rupture in trust often results in a breakdown of boundaries within a relationship. To rebuild trust, it is vital to re-establish clear boundaries that both parties can adhere to. This might involve setting new guidelines for transparency, accountability, and personal space. By openly discussing and mutually agreeing upon these boundaries, individuals can begin to rebuild trust slowly and organically. However, it is essential to ensure that these boundaries are fair, reasonable, and genuinely designed to keep the relationship healthy rather than acting as punitive measures.

3. Consistency and Reliability:

Actions speak louder than words, especially when it comes to rebuilding trust. The person who caused the betrayal must consistently demonstrate their commitment to change through their actions. Consistency and reliability are vital in rebuilding trust, as they signal a sincere desire to repair the relationship. By following through on promises, being punctual, and maintaining honesty, the person who caused the rupture can gradually rebuild trust over time. It is crucial to remember that trust is earned through consistent actions, not simply made through empty words.

4. Patience and Understanding:

Rebuilding trust takes time, and it is essential for both parties to remain patient and understanding throughout the process. The person who has been betrayed should understand that healing cannot happen overnight, and it requires a deep understanding of the complexity of emotions involved. It is normal to experience setbacks and moments of doubt along the way. On the other hand, the person who caused the betrayal must also be patient and understanding, allowing their partner to heal at their own pace and being open to answering any questions or concerns that may arise during this delicate period.

5. Seeking Professional Help:

In some instances, healing relationship ruptures after betrayals may prove to be too challenging to tackle alone. Seeking the guidance of a professional therapist or counselor can provide an impartial viewpoint, facilitate healthy communication, and offer tools for navigating through the tumultuous journey of healing. Professional help can provide individuals with valuable insights and strategies that may not have been previously considered. Remember, there is no shame in seeking assistance, as it demonstrates a genuine commitment to rebuilding the relationship.

6. Cultivating Emotional Resilience:

Both parties involved in the healing process must cultivate emotional resilience to overcome the hardships experienced due to the betrayal. Building resilience involves developing self-awareness, self-compassion, and practicing coping mechanisms that promote emotional well-being. Engaging in activities such as journaling, practicing mindfulness, or seeking support from friends and family can be instrumental in the process. By fostering emotional resilience, individuals can better manage triggers and setbacks, allowing for a more robust foundation upon which trust can be rebuilt.

Healing relationship ruptures after betrayals is an arduous journey that demands immense effort, empathy, and a genuine desire to repair the damage done.

By implementing techniques such as honest communication, re-establishing boundaries, consistency, patience, seeking professional help, and cultivating emotional resilience, individuals can pave the pathway towards healing and rebuilding trust. It is vital to remember that forgiveness and healing are unique to each individual, and not all relationships can mend after a betrayal.

However, by staying committed to the process and valuing the growth and transformation that can arise from such challenges, individuals can create a healthier, stronger, and more resilient bond with their loved ones.

External Stresses and Relationship Strain: Managing outside pressures without allowing them to undermine your bond

In every relationship, there are bound to be external stresses that can potentially strain the bond between partners. These stresses can arise from various sources, such as work-related pressures, financial difficulties, or even societal expectations. However, it is essential to recognize and manage these outside pressures in a healthy and constructive manner to prevent them from negatively impacting the relationship. In this chapter, we will explore the different external stresses that couples often face and provide strategies for maintaining a strong bond in the face of these challenges.

1. Identifying External Stresses:

The first step in managing external stresses is to identify their sources accurately. External stresses can originate from various domains of life, including professional, social, and family circles. It is crucial to understand that external pressures are often unavoidable, but it is how we handle them that determines their impact on our relationship. By recognizing and acknowledging these stresses, we can approach them proactively and prevent them from taking a toll on our partnership.

2. Work-Related Pressures:

One of the most common sources of external stress in relationships is work-related pressures. In today's fast-paced and demanding work environment, it is challenging to strike a balance between career goals and personal life. Long working hours, deadlines, and job insecurities can result in exhaustion and strain in a relationship. To manage such stresses effectively, it is crucial for partners to communicate openly about their work-related concerns and explore strategies to support each other. Setting boundaries between work and personal life, prioritizing quality time together, and finding shared hobbies or activities can help alleviate work-related tensions.

3. Financial Difficulties:

Another significant external stress that can strain a relationship is financial instability. Money-related issues, such as debt, unemployment, or disagreements over financial decisions, can create immense strain and discord. It is essential for couples to establish open and honest communication around financial matters. By creating a budget together, setting financial goals, and finding ways to support each other during challenging times, couples can reduce financial stress and work towards long-term stability.

4. Societal Expectations:

Societal expectations can also add strain to a relationship. Pressure to conform to societal norms, cultural practices, or gender roles can significantly impact couples' dynamics. It is crucial for partners to understand and respect each other's individuality and find a balance between societal expectations and personal values. Open and respectful communication about expectations and the implementation of shared decision-making can help navigate societal pressures and strengthen the bond between partners.

5. Family and Social Circle:

Family dynamics and the influence of the social circle can introduce external stressors into a relationship. Interference from family members, differences in upbringing, or conflicts with friends can put a strain on a couple's bond. It is important to establish clear boundaries and communicate openly with family members and close friends, making it clear that your relationship deserves respect and support. Regular and honest discussion with your partner about expectations regarding involvement with extended family and friends can help navigate these challenging situations effectively.

6. Balancing Individual Needs:

While managing external stresses, it is crucial not to neglect one's own individual needs and personal growth. Each partner must find a way to balance their personal aspirations and desires with the needs of the relationship. Encouraging and supporting each other's individual growth, pursuing personal hobbies, and maintaining a healthy sense of self can contribute positively to the relationship's overall strength and resilience.

7. Seeking External Support:

Sometimes, when external stresses become overwhelming, seeking external support can be immensely beneficial. Couples can opt for relationship counseling or therapy, which provides a safe space to discuss challenges, improve communication, and develop effective strategies to manage external pressures. Seeking support from trusted friends, family members, or mentors who can provide guidance and perspective can also be helpful.

8. Building Resilience:

Lastly, building resilience within the relationship is vital to handling external stresses. Resilience enables couples to adapt and grow stronger even in the face of challenges. By practicing effective communication, problem-solving skills, and supporting each other through both good times and bad, couples can build a foundation of resilience. Developing shared rituals, maintaining physical and emotional intimacy, and expressing gratitude towards each other regularly are ways to foster resilience and nurture the bond over time.

Managing external stresses and preventing them from undermining a relationship requires effort, patience, and understanding. By recognizing the sources of external stress, developing effective strategies to cope, and seeking external support when needed, couples can navigate these challenges and emerge stronger together. Remember, a strong bond can weather any storm, and by proactively managing external stresses, couples can ensure their relationship remains resilient in the face of adversity.

Chapter 4: Building Together for the Future

In this chapter, we delve into the importance of collaboration and the power it holds in shaping a brighter future for individuals, organizations, and society as a whole. We explore the concept of building together, the underlying principles of successful collaboration, and the transformative impact it can have on both personal and collective growth. Through real-life examples and thought-provoking insights, we aim to inspire readers to embrace collaboration as a guiding principle in their own lives and work towards creating a better future for all.

The Power of Collaboration:

Collaboration, at its core, is a process where individuals or groups come together, collectively contributing their skills, knowledge, and resources towards a common goal. It is a fundamental pillar of progress and development, enabling us to pool our strengths and bring about positive change on a much grander scale.

One of the key benefits of collaboration is that it promotes diversity of thought. When individuals with different backgrounds and experiences join forces, there is an inherent richness and variety of ideas that emerge. These diverse perspectives lead to enhanced problem-solving capabilities and significantly increase the chances of finding innovative and creative solutions to complex challenges.

Moreover, collaboration fosters a sense of shared ownership and commitment. When people work together towards a common purpose, they are more invested and motivated to deliver results. This shared responsibility creates a strong bond among collaborators, empowering them to overcome obstacles and persevere in the face of adversity.

Building Together: Principles of Successful Collaboration:

Successful collaboration does not occur by chance; it requires a thoughtful approach and adherence to certain principles. Let's explore some key principles that can guide us towards successful collaborative efforts:

1. Common Vision and Goals: The foundation of any collaboration lies in defining a common vision and goals that all participants enthusiastically align with. This shared purpose serves as a driving force, uniting collaborators towards a singular direction and sense of mission.

2. Trust and Respect: Building trust and fostering mutual respect is

crucial for effective collaboration. It involves acknowledging and valuing diverse perspectives, actively listening to others, and treating each collaborator with dignity. Trust creates a safe space that encourages open communication and encourages the exploration of new ideas.

3. Clear Communication Channels: Transparent and open communication is vital for collaboration to thrive. Establishing clear communication channels, whether through regular meetings, online platforms, or other mediums, ensures that stakeholders are informed, engaged, and given the opportunity to contribute and provide feedback.

4. Shared Decision-Making: A collaborative endeavor must involve shared decision-making processes. While each participant brings unique expertise, the collective wisdom and consensus-building through inclusive decision-making lead to well-rounded solutions that benefit all.

5. Effective Conflict Resolution: Conflicts and disagreements are inevitable in any collaboration. Nurturing a culture that effectively handles and resolves conflicts is essential. Encouraging open dialogue, active listening, and seeking compromises can turn conflicts into opportunities for growth and deeper understanding.

Collaboration for Personal Growth:

The power of collaboration extends beyond organizations and can greatly impact personal growth and development. Engaging in collaborative efforts enables individuals to broaden their skill sets, deepen their knowledge, and expand their networks.

When collaborating with others, individuals have the opportunity to learn from different perspectives, unlocking new insights, and enhancing their understanding of the world. By stepping outside their comfort zones and engaging in meaningful dialogue, individuals can develop adaptability, empathy, and stronger interpersonal skills.

Furthermore, collaboration encourages individuals to share their strengths and leverage the strengths of others. By recognizing and valuing their own unique contributions, individuals gain a sense of self-assurance and become more willing to embrace growth and take on new challenges.

Collaboration: Organizations and Society:

Just as collaboration impacts individuals, it also plays a pivotal role in shaping organizations and society at large. Successful collaborations within organizations can lead to increased productivity, improved employee satisfaction, and innovation. By fostering an environment that encourages collaboration, organizations tap into the diverse talents of their workforce and create a culture of collective success.

On a societal level, collaborative efforts are catalysts for change. Throughout history, countless examples exist of collaborative movements that have led to groundbreaking advancements in various fields. Whether it be scientific breakthroughs, social reforms, or global initiatives, collaboration has been the driving force behind transformative change. By working together, societies can address pressing challenges such as poverty, inequality, and climate change, ensuring a brighter future for all.

Chapter 4 has explored the transformative power of collaboration in shaping a brighter future for individuals, organizations, and society as a whole. We have examined the principles of successful collaboration and emphasized the importance of building together towards common goals. Through collaboration, we can harness the diverse perspectives, expertise, and collective wisdom of individuals to create innovative solutions and effect meaningful change. By embracing collaboration in our personal and professional lives, we can truly build a future that is inclusive, sustainable, and prosperous for all.

Setting Relationship Goals: Mapping out a future that reflects both partners' aspirations

Relationships are a beautiful journey that requires effort, understanding, and compromise. When two individuals come together to form a partnership, it is essential to have a shared vision of the future. Mapping out relationship goals that align with both partners' aspirations lays the foundation for a successful and fulfilling journey ahead. In this chapter, we will explore the importance of setting relationship goals, how to identify individual aspirations, and the process of developing shared goals that serve as guiding pillars for the relationship's growth.

Understanding the Significance of Relationship Goals:

Relationship goals serve as a roadmap, providing direction and purpose to a couple's journey together. When both partners are invested in setting goals, it helps to create a solid and secure foundation based on shared values and aspirations. By setting goals, couples can foster open communication, understanding, and trust, allowing them to navigate challenges and celebrate their achievements as a team. This chapter aims to equip you with the knowledge and tools to identify and set relationship goals that will cultivate happiness and longevity in your partnership.

Identifying Individual Aspirations:

Before diving into shared relationship goals, it is essential for each partner to reflect on their individual aspirations. To create a harmonious and balanced relationship, it is crucial to understand oneself and one's desires fully. Take some time to reflect on your personal ambitions in various areas of life, such as career, personal growth, family, and hobbies. Write them down and seek clarity within yourself. Identifying your aspirations will enable you to communicate them effectively to your partner, ultimately helping you establish shared goals.

Effective Communication:

To map out a future that reflects both partners' aspirations, effective communication is of utmost importance. Communication forms the backbone of any successful relationship, and setting goals is no exception. Create a safe and non-judgmental space where both partners can express their thoughts and desires openly. Actively listen, show empathy, and validate each other's feelings. By doing so, you create an environment of trust and understanding, enhancing the bond between you and your partner.

Developing Shared Goals:

Once you have individually identified your aspirations and established open communication, it is time to delve into developing shared goals. Shared goals are rooted in compromise and collaboration, combining the desires and aspirations of both partners. Begin by discussing your individual goals with each other, exploring the areas where your aspirations align and where they differ. This process allows you to identify common ground and understand each other better.

During goal setting, it is essential to focus on the key areas that significantly impact the relationship. These may include financial stability, aspects of personal growth, family planning, career development, travel, or creating a comfortable home environment. Prioritize these areas and discuss what achieving these goals will mean for both of you. Remember to be flexible, open-minded, and willing to adjust your thoughts and expectations to find middle ground that honors both partners' aspirations.

Setting Realistic and Attainable Goals:

While dreaming big is admirable, it is crucial to set realistic and attainable goals within your relationship. Unrealistic expectations can strain the partnership and lead to disappointment. Discuss with your partner what is feasible for both of you given your current circumstances and future plans. Consider the resources available, such as time, finances, and emotional capacity, to set goals that are achievable and sustainable.

Creating a Timetable:

Setting a timetable helps turn aspirations into actionable goals. Without a timeline, goals may remain vague and indefinite, leading to frustration or lack of motivation. Collaborate with your partner to establish realistic timelines for achieving your shared goals. This ensures that both partners stay motivated while holding each other accountable. Remember to be flexible and understanding, as circumstances may change, requiring adjustments to the timetable.

Tracking Progress and Celebrating Achievements:

Once you have set your shared goals and established a timeline, it is vital to track progress and celebrate achievements along the way. Regularly assess your progress, and communicate with your partner about how you are both feeling. Acknowledge the steps taken, celebrate each milestone, and learn from any setbacks. By celebrating achievements, you reinforce the joy and satisfaction of working together towards a shared future.

Revisiting and Reassessing Goals:

Relationships and individuals evolve over time, making it necessary to revisit and reassess your shared goals regularly. Life circumstances, personal growth, and unforeseen situations may require adjustments to the goals you set initially. This does not mean failure; instead, it reflects the adaptability and commitment to growth within your relationship. Be open to reevaluating your goals together, and ensure they continue to align with both partners' evolving aspirations.

In this chapter, we explored the significance of setting relationship goals that reflect both partners' aspirations. Setting goals provides direction, purpose, and growth opportunities within a relationship. By identifying individual aspirations, cultivating open communication, and developing shared goals, couples lay the foundation for a successful and fulfilling partnership. Remember that the process of setting goals is ongoing, requiring flexibility, understanding, and adaptability. Through collaboration and commitment, you and your partner can embark on a journey that reflects the best of each other while achieving personal and shared aspirations.

Financial Bridges: Strategies for managing and merging finances effectively

Managing finances can be a daunting task, especially when it involves merging finances with a partner or spouse. However, it is a crucial aspect of building a strong foundation for a successful life together. This chapter aims to provide practical strategies and tips for managing and merging finances effectively, ensuring a harmonious financial journey. From open communication to setting shared goals, we will explore various methods to establish financial bridges that will withstand the test of time.

1. Open and Transparent Communication:

The first strategy for managing and merging finances effectively is open and transparent communication. Both partners must be willing to discuss their individual financial situations openly, including any debts, investments, or financial obligations. It is crucial to develop an environment where both parties feel comfortable sharing their thoughts and concerns without judgment.

When merging finances, it is necessary to have a clear understanding of each other's financial goals and expectations. Discussing financial aspirations, such as buying a house or saving for retirement, allows both partners to align their goals and create a shared vision for the future. Regular check-ins and open conversations about finances can prevent misunderstandings or surprises down the road.

2. Combine and Separate Finances:

One common question when merging finances is whether to combine all accounts or keep separate accounts. There is no one-size-fits-all answer to this question as it depends on individual preferences and circumstances. However, a commonly adopted approach is to combine certain aspects of finances while keeping some independence.

A practical strategy is combining essential expenses such as rent or mortgage payments, utilities, and groceries into a joint account. Each partner contributes a predetermined amount to cover these shared expenses. This approach promotes a sense of joint responsibility and ensures fair participation while still allowing financial independence for discretionary spending.

Maintaining separate accounts for personal expenses, such as hobbies, entertainment, or gifts, can give both partners the freedom to manage their discretionary funds without constant scrutiny. It is essential to establish a discretionary budget that each individual can spend without consulting the other, promoting a sense of personal freedom and accountability.

3. Establishing a Joint Budget:

Creating a joint budget is a crucial step towards managing finances effectively. A joint budget provides an overview of income, expenses, and financial goals shared by both partners. It allows for better financial planning and ensures that both individuals are on the same page when it comes to financial decisions.

To create a joint budget, start by listing all sources of income from both partners. Include salary, bonuses, investment returns, or any other regular income streams. Next, list all expenses, including fixed expenses like rent or mortgage payments, utilities, and loan repayments, as well as variable expenses like groceries, dining out, and entertainment.
The joint budget should take into account short-term and long-term financial goals shared by both partners. This includes saving for emergencies, retirement funds, future family planning, or any other aspirations. Allocate a portion of your joint income towards these goals, ensuring regular contributions and monitoring progress.

4. Consider a Joint Account for Joint Goals:
While maintaining separate accounts for personal expenses is

beneficial, it is essential to consider opening a joint account specifically for joint goals. This could be a savings account for a down payment on a house, a vacation fund, or any other shared financial objective.

Contributing to a joint account regularly demonstrates commitment towards shared financial goals. Set up automatic transfers from individual accounts to the joint account to ensure consistent progress. Regularly review the joint account's progress and adjust contributions if necessary to maintain alignment with the set goals.

5. Share Responsibility for Financial Duties:

Managing finances effectively requires shared responsibility and an equal division of financial duties. It is essential to establish clear roles and responsibilities for tasks such as budgeting, bill payments, and investment management.

Dividing financial responsibilities not only reduces the burden on one individual but also promotes trust and accountability. To achieve this, have a conversation about individual strengths and interests when it comes to financial tasks. For example, one partner may be more inclined towards tracking expenses and creating budgets, while the other may excel at investment management or financial research.

Regularly review the division of financial duties to ensure a fair and balanced arrangement. This will help avoid any resentment or misunderstandings in the long run and enhance overall financial harmony.

6. Plan for Contingencies:

Life is unpredictable, and planning for contingencies is a vital aspect of effective financial management. Both partners must discuss and plan for unexpected events such as job loss, medical emergencies, or other financial hardships.

Building an emergency fund should be a shared priority. Set a monthly contribution to this fund based on your joint budget and make it a non-negotiable aspect of your finances. Ideally, aim to have enough savings to cover at least six months' worth of essential expenses. Regularly review and adjust the emergency fund based on changes in income or expenses.

Additionally, consider other forms of financial protection such as life insurance, disability insurance, or critical illness insurance. These insurance policies can provide peace of mind and financial security in times of need.

Managing and merging finances effectively is a continuous process that requires open communication, trust, and shared responsibility. By implementing the strategies discussed in this chapter, couples can build a solid financial foundation that will support their shared goals and aspirations.

Regularly reassess your financial situation, adjust your joint budget, and set new goals together as your circumstances change.

Remember that financial bridges are built on trust, understanding, and mutual respect. With a shared vision and effective financial management, you can navigate any challenges that come your way and create a prosperous future together.

Growing as a Duo: Approaches to personal development that strengthen the relationship

In any successful relationship, personal growth and development are essential aspects that truly strengthen the bond between individuals. When two people commit to sharing their lives and building a future together, it is crucial for both partners to embark on personal development journeys that complement and enhance each other. By focusing on personal growth as a duo, couples can create a strong foundation for their relationship, fostering individual happiness and collective growth. In this chapter, we will explore various approaches to personal development that can be undertaken by couples to strengthen their bond and create a flourishing partnership.

1. Communication: The Key to Understanding and Empathy

Effective communication forms the cornerstone of any healthy relationship. To cultivate personal development as a duo, couples should prioritize open and honest communication channels. Active listening, expressing emotions, and empathizing with each other's experiences are fundamental aspects of building understanding and trust.

To strengthen communication, couples can engage in regular dialogue sessions, preferably in a calm and relaxed environment. These sessions should be dedicated to discussing concerns, aspirations, and personal growth goals openly. By engaging in open conversations, partners can better understand each other's needs, desires, and intentions, fostering a deeper emotional connection.

2. Shared Goals: Building a Common Vision

To grow individually and as a duo, it is essential to establish shared goals and aspirations. By aligning their visions for the future, couples can embark on a collective journey of personal development. Identifying common dreams and objectives not only enhances the bond but also provides a powerful motivator for growth.

Creating shared goals involves identifying individual aspirations and finding areas where both partners can contribute towards a common purpose. These goals can range from career development and financial stability to personal hobbies and travel plans. By actively working together to achieve these goals, couples can nurture a sense of shared accomplishment and celebrate mutual success.

3. Mutual Support: Encouraging Growth

Supporting each other's personal growth endeavors is vital in any relationship. By offering encouragement, motivation, and a safe space for exploration, couples can empower each other to pursue their passions and achieve personal milestones. Mutual support creates an environment of trust and provides a foundation for individual and collective growth.

To foster mutual support, partners should actively engage in each other's aspirations. This can involve attending workshops, classes, or seminars together, or simply lending an ear to discuss progress and challenges. Establishing a routine of providing feedback, appreciation, and constructive criticism can also enhance personal development while strengthening the relationship.

4. Individual Space: Nurturing Independence

While growing as a duo is important, it is equally crucial for partners to maintain their individuality. Allowing space for personal interests, hobbies, and friendships helps nurture independence and self-discovery. Embracing individuality not only enhances personal growth but also brings new experiences and perspectives to the relationship.

Creating individual space involves setting boundaries and establishing periods of personal time or engaging in solitary activities. By respecting each other's need for independence, couples can cultivate a sense of self and encourage personal growth. This space also provides an opportunity for partners to reflect and introspect, contributing to their overall well-being.

5. Continuous Learning: Expanding Horizons Together

Learning is a lifelong journey, and couples can significantly benefit from engaging in continuous learning together. By exploring new subjects, acquiring new skills, or pursuing joint interests, partners can expand their knowledge and horizons. Shared learning experiences contribute to personal development and serve as a bonding factor within the relationship.

To foster continuous learning, couples can enroll in classes, attend lectures, or even embark on travel adventures that offer opportunities for learning and exploration. The process of acquiring knowledge together not only deepens the bond but also creates shared memories and experiences that strengthen the partnership.

6. Conflict Resolution: A Pathway to Growth and Understanding

Conflict is an inevitable part of any relationship, and how couples handle conflicts determines the strength of their bond. Instead of avoiding conflicts, couples should view them as opportunities for growth and understanding. Embracing conflict resolution techniques helps partners develop emotional intelligence and strengthen their connection.

To effectively resolve conflicts, couples can practice active listening, expressing vulnerability, and embracing compromise. Taking the time to understand each other's perspectives and finding common ground fosters trust, respect, and personal growth. Conflict resolution also enables partners to learn from their experiences, ultimately enhancing their communication and problem-solving skills.

7. Building a Support Network: Surrounding Yourself with Positive Influences

While personal development within the relationship is crucial, expanding the support network beyond the partnership can also contribute to growth. Encouraging each other to build relationships outside the couple allows for diverse perspectives, external guidance, and an additional source of motivation and inspiration. Cultivating a supportive network involves engaging with friends, family, mentors, or support groups that align with individual passions and goals. These connections can offer fresh insights, create opportunities for collaboration, and enhance personal growth by broadening horizons and exposing partners to new ideas and experiences.

By embracing personal development as a duo, couples lay the foundation for a strong, sustainable, and fulfilling relationship. Prioritizing open communication, shared goals, mutual support, and individual space creates an environment conducive to personal growth. Additionally, continuous learning, conflict resolution, and building a supportive network contribute to overall relationship enhancement. Remember, personal growth is not a destination but a lifelong journey, and embarking on this journey together can create a vibrant and flourishing partnership.

Planning for Challenges Ahead: Proactively fortifying your relationship against potential future strains

In all relationships, there are bound to be challenges that arise from time to time. Whether it's external factors like work pressure, financial difficulties, or internal conflicts stemming from differing perspectives, learning to navigate these challenges can greatly strengthen your bond as a couple. However, simply reacting to challenges when they occur may not always be the most effective approach. In this chapter, we will explore the importance of proactive planning and fortifying your relationship against potential future strains.

1. The Power of Anticipation

As the famous saying goes, "Prevention is better than cure." This sentiment holds true not only in healthcare but also in safeguarding the health of your relationship. By anticipating potential future strains, you can effectively prepare and brace yourselves for the challenges that lie ahead. This proactive approach demonstrates your commitment to your partner and your relationship, showing that you are willing to put in the effort to ensure its longevity and success.

2. Communication as the Foundation

Open and honest communication is the bedrock upon which a strong relationship is built. In preparing for future strains, it is crucial to establish a safe and comfortable space where both partners can freely express their concerns, fears, and aspirations. Engage in regular conversations about your goals, dreams, and expectations for the future, allowing you to gain a deeper understanding of each other and find common ground.

3. Identifying Potential Strains

To proactively fortify your relationship, it is essential to identify potential strains that may arise in the future. Consider both external and internal factors that may impact your relationship negatively. External factors can include career changes, financial difficulties, health issues, or family problems, while internal factors might involve communication breakdowns, emotional disconnect, or diverging life goals. By recognizing these potential strains, you are better equipped to develop strategies to overcome them.

4. Creating a Shared Vision

In planning for the challenges ahead, it is vital to create a shared vision for your relationship. This shared vision acts as a guiding light, helping you navigate through difficult times. Sit down together and discuss your individual aspirations, hopes, and dreams. Find commonalities and work towards aligning your future aspirations as a couple. This exercise will foster a sense of togetherness and establish a strong foundation from which to face future challenges.

5. Developing Conflict Resolution Strategies

Conflicts are an inevitable part of any relationship. To fortify your relationship against potential future strains, it is crucial to develop effective conflict resolution strategies. This involves learning how to approach conflicts with empathy, active listening, and a willingness to compromise. Utilize "I" statements to express your feelings without blaming your partner, and practice reflective listening to ensure that both partners feel heard and understood.

6. Building Emotional Resilience

Emotional resilience plays a significant role in withstanding the strains of a relationship. By focusing on building emotional resilience together, you strengthen your bond and develop a shared understanding of how to support each other during difficult times.

This can be achieved through exercises such as practicing gratitude, engaging in stress-reducing activities, or seeking professional help when needed. Building emotional resilience equips you both with the tools to face potential future strains head-on.

7. Regular Check-Ins

Proactively fortifying your relationship requires consistent effort and open lines of communication. Implement regular check-ins to reassess your shared vision, progress, and any potential strains that may have emerged. The frequency of these check-ins will depend on your unique circumstances, but aim for at least one check-in every few months. See these check-ins as opportunities to celebrate successes, address challenges, and realign your goals as a couple.

8. Seeking Support and Guidance

No relationship exists in isolation, and seeking support and guidance from trusted sources can greatly enhance your ability to fortify your relationship. Consider attending relationship workshops, seeking couples therapy, or reading books on effective communication and relationship building. By investing in your relationship through these resources, you demonstrate a shared commitment to overcoming potential future strains.

9. Embracing Flexibility and Adaptability

As life unfolds, it is vital to embrace flexibility and adaptability within your relationship. Accept the fact that circumstances may change, and adjustments may be necessary along the way. By acknowledging this reality, you can mitigate potential strains that arise from resistance to change and foster an environment that supports growth and transformation.

10. Celebrating Milestones and Achievements

Lastly, amidst the planning and preparation for potential strains, do not forget to celebrate milestones and achievements together. Recognize the progress you have made as a couple and cherish the moments of joy along the way. By acknowledging and appreciating each other's accomplishments, you strengthen the bond between you and remind yourselves of the love and happiness you share.

In summary, taking a proactive approach to fortifying your relationship against potential future strains is a powerful way to ensure its long-term success. By communicating openly, identifying potential strains, building emotional resilience, and seeking support, you can navigate future challenges together with strength and grace. Remember, relationships are constantly evolving, and by preparing for what lies ahead, you can create a bond that thrives even in the face of adversity.

Chapter 5: Nurturing Relationships Through Life's Stages

Life is a journey filled with countless experiences that shape us into the individuals we become. One of the most vital aspects of this lifelong expedition is the relationships we cultivate along the way. Relationships, whether they be familial, romantic, or platonic, provide us with the support, love, and companionship that enrich our lives. In this chapter, we will explore the importance of nurturing relationships through life's various stages, understanding the challenges that arise, and discovering strategies to cultivate thriving connections that endure the tests of time.

Section 1: Building Foundations in Childhood

Our childhood experiences lay the groundwork for the relationships we form later in life. It is during this early stage that we learn the importance of trust, empathy, and shared connection. The unconditional love and support from our family members serve as the blueprint for how we relate to others in the future. As children, we eagerly explore our surroundings, making friends effortlessly and finding comfort in the company of others. The innocence of childhood often allows for genuine connections to blossom.

However, childhood is not without its fair share of challenges. Sibling rivalries, parental conflicts, and unforeseen traumas can disrupt the harmony we long for. But it is through these difficulties that we learn resilience and the ability to navigate complex emotions within relationships. Understanding that forgiveness, compassion, and open communication are essential tools in building lasting connections can help guide us through the uncertainties of childhood.

Section 2: Navigating Friendships and Romance in Adolescence

Adolescence is a time of tremendous growth and self-discovery. During this phase, friendships play a pivotal role in shaping our identities and teaching us valuable lessons about loyalty, compromise, and accountability. Our friends become confidants, partners in mischief, and a support system as we navigate the challenges of this transitional period. Through shared experiences, we learn the importance of empathy, and the ability to celebrate one another's successes and support each other during hardships.

Romantic relationships also emerge during adolescence, introducing a new level of vulnerability and intimacy. Exploring our feelings and developing emotional bonds with a romantic partner teaches us the art of compromise, communication, and understanding. However, the intensity of the emotions experienced during this period can also give rise to heartbreak, jealousy, and insecurity. Learning to manage these emotions and communicate effectively can set a strong foundation for healthy relationships in adulthood.

Section 3: Nurturing Relationships in Adulthood

Adulthood brings with it a plethora of responsibilities and challenges that can impact our ability to nurture relationships. From career aspirations to raising a family, the demands of everyday life can leave us feeling overwhelmed and disconnected. However, investing time and effort into our relationships remains essential for our well-being.

In adulthood, strong bonds with family members become even more critical as we navigate the trials and tribulations of adult life. Sustaining relationships with parents, siblings, and extended family provides us with a sense of belonging, support, and wisdom. Despite the busyness of life, making a deliberate effort to prioritize family ties ensures that our relationships have the resilience to withstand the test of time.

Moreover, adulthood presents opportunities to build romantic partnerships that evolve into lifelong commitments. The ability to cultivate love, trust, and shared goals becomes the cornerstone of a fulfilling and enduring relationship. Understanding the significance of compromise, effective communication, and maintaining intimacy promotes a strong and thriving partnership.

Section 4: Nurturing Relationships Through Parenthood

Parenthood introduces a whole new level of nurturing relationships as we transition from being cared for to caring for others. Becoming a parent is a transformative experience that requires selflessness, patience, and unconditional love. Building a strong foundation with our children involves providing a safe and nurturing environment, fostering open communication, and being a consistent source of support.

Navigating the challenges of parenting while maintaining a healthy relationship with a partner can be demanding. Balancing the needs of children alongside the needs of a romantic relationship requires effective communication, shared responsibilities, and intentional quality time as a couple. By prioritizing the bond with our life partner, we ensure that the love and support for our children stems from a strong and connected base.

Section 5: Cultivating Relationships in Later Stages of Life
As we enter the later stages of life, our focus often shifts towards introspection and reflection. However, nurturing relationships during this phase of life remains crucial for our overall well-being. As we age, our friendships become enriched by shared memories, wisdom, and mutual support. These relationships offer us companionship and emotional sustenance during times of transition and loss.

Furthermore, nurturing relationships with our adult children and grandchildren becomes a source of joy and fulfillment. By staying involved in their lives and providing guidance and wisdom, we can create lasting bonds that traverse generations. Sharing life experiences and imparting lessons learned can bring strength and connectivity to these relationships.

Nurturing relationships throughout life's stages is an ongoing endeavor that requires effort, understanding, and adaptability. From childhood to later stages of life, the ability to cultivate meaningful connections enriches our lives and contributes to our overall happiness and well-being.

By understanding the challenges unique to each stage and implementing strategies for effective communication, empathy, and support, we can develop relationships that endure the tests of time, offering us love, companionship, and a sense of belonging.

Bridging the Early Years: Making the most of the honeymoon phase and setting a strong foundation

The early years of a child's life are crucial for their overall development. It is in this time frame, often referred to as the honeymoon phase, that children are most receptive to learning and forming new connections. As educators, parents, and caregivers, it is our responsibility to make the most of this phase and provide children with a strong foundation on which they can build their future. In this chapter, we will explore various strategies and approaches to effectively bridge the early years, ensuring optimal growth and development for every child.

Understanding the Honeymoon Phase:

The honeymoon phase is a term used to describe the initial period when children are exposed to a new environment, such as a school or a daycare setting. During this phase, children are generally excited, curious, and eager to explore their surroundings. They are highly receptive to instructions, social interactions, and learning opportunities. It is crucial for educators and caregivers to recognize and utilize this phase effectively to create a positive and enriching experience for children.

Creating a Nurturing Environment:

A nurturing environment plays a pivotal role in making the most of the honeymoon phase. By providing a safe and welcoming space, children can develop a sense of belonging and trust in their caregivers. This environment may include cozy and well-organized classrooms, age-appropriate toys and materials, and a positive color scheme that promotes a sense of calmness and comfort. Additionally, ensuring a routine that balances play, rest, social interaction, and learning activities can further enhance children's overall experience.

Building Positive Relationships:

Positive relationships with caregivers and educators are crucial during the early years. These relationships foster a sense of security, encourage emotional and social development, and provide a foundation for future interactions. Taking the time to build strong connections with each child, understanding their individual needs, and providing responsive care are essential steps in bridging the early years successfully. Engaging in conversations, active listening, and expressing empathy can go a long way in building these fundamental relationships.

Tailoring Instruction:

During the honeymoon phase, children are more receptive to learning. Educators and caregivers must take advantage of this period by tailoring instruction to meet individual needs. By adopting a child-centered approach and embracing various learning styles, educators can create an inclusive environment that accommodates every child's unique abilities and interests. This individualized instruction allows children to explore their potential, build confidence, and set a strong foundation for future academic success.

Promoting Language Development:

Language and communication skills are fundamental for cognitive, social, and emotional growth in early childhood. The honeymoon phase provides an opportune time to focus on promoting language development. Encouraging verbal interactions, storytelling, reading aloud, and engaging children in conversations can enhance their vocabulary, comprehension, and expressive abilities. Additionally, incorporating songs, rhymes, and gestures into daily routines can make language learning engaging and fun.

Encouraging Play-Based Learning:

Play is the primary medium through which young children explore, learn, and make sense of the world around them. During the honeymoon phase, educators should utilize play-based learning methodologies to foster holistic development. Offering open-ended toys, providing opportunities for imaginative play, and setting up various learning centers can stimulate the different domains of a child's development, such as cognitive, social, and motor skills. Play not only enhances creativity and problem-solving abilities but also allows children to develop essential social skills such as cooperation, empathy, and conflict resolution.

Incorporating Sensory Experiences:

The early years are a period of rapid sensory development. By providing rich sensory experiences, we can enhance children's cognitive and neurological growth. Incorporating sensory play, such as sand, water, and playdough, can stimulate fine motor skills, creativity, and cognitive processes. Additionally, incorporating music, textures, scents, and tastes further engages children's senses, enabling them to explore and learn in a multi-dimensional manner.

Promoting Emotional Regulation:

Emotional regulation is a critical skill that children develop during the early years. Educators and caregivers can play a significant role in guiding children towards healthy emotional development. By providing a safe space for children to express and understand their emotions, we can foster emotional intelligence. Encouraging mindfulness activities, implementing calming strategies, and teaching age-appropriate techniques for self-regulation can empower children to navigate their emotions effectively. This, in turn, lays a robust foundation for positive mental health and well-being.

Bridging the early years effectively involves making the most of the honeymoon phase and setting a strong foundation in children's overall development. By creating a nurturing environment, building positive relationships, tailoring instruction, promoting language development, encouraging play-based learning, incorporating sensory experiences, and promoting emotional regulation, educators and caregivers can ensure optimal growth and development for every child. Embracing this responsibility with care and dedication is essential as we shape the future success and well-being of our youngest learners.

Mid-relationship Renewals: Reinvigorating and reaffirming your connection over time

In the journey of love, relationships often go through different phases. The initial spark of romance and excitement may fade over time, leaving both partners yearning for a deeper connection. However, the natural progression of relationships does not mean that the love between partners diminishes; it simply means that the relationship needs a mid-relationship renewal. This chapter will explore various strategies to reinvigorate and reaffirm your connection, helping you reignite the spark and create a stronger bond with your partner.

Understanding the Mid-Relationship Phase:

The mid-relationship phase is an inevitable part of every relationship, where the initial excitement mellows down, and routine starts to settle in. At this stage, partners may experience a sense of longing for the early days when everything felt new and exciting. It's important to acknowledge that this phase is entirely normal and does not imply a decrease in affection or love between partners. Instead, it signals an opportunity for growth and the deepening of your connection.

Open Communication:

One of the most crucial aspects of a healthy relationship is maintaining open and honest communication. In the mid-relationship phase, it becomes even more vital to have heartfelt conversations with your partner. Share your feelings, concerns, and desires openly, and encourage your partner to do the same. Through effective communication, you can better understand each other's needs and work together to rekindle the flame that brought you together in the first place.

Rediscover Each Other:

In the hustle and bustle of everyday life, it's easy to lose sight of the uniqueness of your partner. Take the time to reintroduce yourselves, both as a couple and as individuals. Engage in activities that you both enjoy, and explore new hobbies and adventures together. By rediscovering each other, you can find common ground and reignite the excitement that once defined your relationship.

Quality Time:

With the demands of work, family, and other commitments, quality time often takes a backseat in relationships. However, spending quality time with your partner is vital for nurturing your connection. Set aside dedicated time to be fully present with each other, whether it's through date nights, weekend getaways, or simply enjoying a quiet evening together. Focus on building emotional intimacy and strengthening your bond.

Embrace Novelty:

Routine can be a relationship killer, as it often leads to boredom and complacency. To counteract this, embrace novelty in your relationship. Engage in activities that are out of the ordinary, try new experiences together, and surprise your partner with gestures of love and affection. By injecting novelty into your relationship, you not only create memorable moments but also reaffirm the dynamism and excitement within your connection.

Intimacy and Physical Affection:

Physical intimacy is a vital component of a healthy relationship. However, as time passes, it's common for physical affection to dwindle. To reignite this aspect of your connection, focus on nurturing intimacy in your relationship. Engage in simple acts of physical affection like cuddling, holding hands, or sharing an intimate embrace. Make an effort to express your love through touch, as it can strengthen the emotional bond between partners.

Shared Goals and Dreams:

Renewing your connection involves looking beyond the present and envisioning a shared future. Take the time to discuss and set shared goals and dreams for your relationship. Working as a team towards a common purpose can reignite the passion and generate a sense of excitement for what lies ahead. These shared goals serve as a reminder of the depth and importance of your partnership.

Adapting and Growing Together:

As individuals, we constantly evolve and change. It's crucial to recognize that both you and your partner will undergo personal growth throughout the course of your relationship. Embrace this growth and strive to adapt and grow together as a couple. Support each other through life's challenges and celebrate each other's achievements. By evolving together, you create a deeper bond that can withstand the tests of time.

While the mid-relationship phase can initially feel disheartening, it shouldn't be seen as a sign of faltering love. Instead, view it as an opportunity for growth, renewal, and relationship improvement. By employing the strategies discussed in this chapter, including open communication, rediscovery, quality time, embracing novelty, physical affection, shared goals, and growth, you can successfully reinvigorate and reaffirm your connection. Remember, relationships require continual effort, but the rewards of a stronger, more loving connection are immeasurable.

Silver Bridges: Understanding and adapting to the challenges and opportunities in long-term relationships

In this chapter, we delve into the complex and evolving nature of long-term relationships. Every relationship experiences its own unique challenges and opportunities as it matures, just like bridges that are built to withstand the tests of time. However, understanding and adapting to these challenges is crucial for building strong and lasting connections. In this regard, we explore the concept of silver bridges, a term coined to symbolize the strength, resilience, and adaptability required to navigate the ever-changing dynamics of long-term partnerships. Let us traverse these silver bridges together, gaining insights into the intricacies of long-term relationships and discovering ways to foster healthier and more fulfilling connections.

The Shifting Dynamic

As relationships progress from the initial stages of euphoria and excitement, a shifting dynamic starts to take hold. The mystery and novelty of the early days give way to familiarity and routine. This transition often leads to a decrease in the level of passion and intensity that marked the beginning, causing some partners to question the stability and longevity of their connection. However, this shift should not be seen as a downfall, but rather an opportunity for growth and deeper understanding.

Recognizing this change is the first step in accepting that long-term relationships are dynamic and require continuous effort and adaptation. Silver bridges understand that the key lies in embracing change, allowing the relationship to evolve naturally while finding ways to maintain the connection and intimacy that initially drew them together.

The Challenges of Communication

Effective communication is the cornerstone of any healthy relationship, yet it remains one of the most significant challenges faced by partners as time passes. Over time, assumptions and lack of clarity can develop, hindering open and honest conversations. Unresolved conflicts, pent-up emotions, and unmet needs can simmer beneath the surface, eroding the foundation of trust and understanding.

Silver bridges recognize the importance of clear and empathetic communication. They understand that active listening, expressing emotions without judgment, and fostering an environment of trust and vulnerability are essential in maintaining strong connections. They are unafraid to address conflicts head-on, seeking resolution rather than pursuing a path of avoidance. By consciously choosing to communicate openly and respectfully, silver bridges bridge the gap that can divide partners over time.

The Erosion of Intimacy

As the years go by, it is common for intimacy to fade or even disappear altogether in long-term relationships. The fire that once burned bright may dwindle as partners become engrossed in their individual lives, careers, and responsibilities. This erosion of intimacy can lead to feelings of loneliness or a sense of drifting apart.

The silver bridges understand the importance of rekindling and nurturing intimacy. They recognize that intimacy encompasses more than just physical connection; it includes emotional closeness and shared experiences. Silver bridges prioritize spending quality time together, engaging in activities that strengthen their emotional and physical bond. From romantic date nights to exploring new hobbies together, these bridges actively seek opportunities to reignite the spark that brought them together initially.

Unearthing Hidden Expectations

Unrealistic expectations often hinder long-term relationships. Partners can fall into the trap of expecting their loved one to fulfill all their needs, fulfill societal norms, or meet impossible standards. These expectations can create pressure and strain on the relationship, leading to disappointment and feelings of inadequacy.

Silver bridges understand that they cannot rely solely on their partner to meet all their needs. They take personal responsibility for their own individual growth, happiness, and fulfillment. They set realistic expectations for themselves and their partner, acknowledging that both are on a journey of continuous growth and change. By building bridges of acceptance and self-awareness, they foster an environment that allows for the genuine expression of self and the freedom to evolve within the relationship.

Embracing Life Transitions

One of the biggest challenges in long-term relationships is navigating life's inevitable transitions together. From starting a family to changing careers or facing health issues, each new phase brings its own set of tests and trials. These transitions can strain even the most solid partnerships, posing questions of identity, purpose, and compatibility.

Silver bridges approach life transitions as opportunities for mutual growth and support. They understand that these moments require flexibility, empathy, and understanding. Rather than viewing these transitions as a threat, they embrace the chance to deepen their connection by actively communicating and fostering a spirit of teamwork. They build bridges of resilience, adapting to change while reinforcing their commitment to one another.

Silver bridges are built on understanding, acceptance, and resilience. They stand as symbols of fortitude and adaptability in the face of the challenges and opportunities that long-term relationships present.

By recognizing the shifting dynamic, embracing effective communication, nurturing intimacy, unearthing hidden expectations, and embracing life transitions, partners can traverse these silver bridges, cultivating relationships that are stronger, more resilient, and more fulfilling. May we embrace the spirit of the silver bridge, allowing it to guide us in our journey toward building long-lasting and fulfilling connections.

Navigating Life Transitions: Supporting each other through major life events, from career changes to family growth

Life is a continuous journey, filled with ups and downs, successes and failures. As we navigate through the different chapters of our lives, we often face major transitions that can be both exhilarating and intimidating. These transitions can range from changes in our careers to the expansion of our families, and they require immense strength and support from those around us. In this chapter, we will explore the importance of supporting one another through these life events, as well as provide practical advice on how to navigate and embrace these transitions with grace and resilience.

Understanding Life Transitions

Life transitions are significant shifts that occur in various areas of our lives, impacting both our personal and professional realms. They can be planned or unexpected, casting a ripple effect on our emotional wellbeing and overall sense of stability. Some common life

transitions include career changes, relocation, marriage, starting a
family, and the loss of a loved one.

It is crucial to recognize that each transition brings about its own set
of unique challenges and opportunities. While some transitions may
be met with excitement and enthusiasm, others can trigger anxiety
and uncertainty. Moreover, the way we perceive and navigate these
transitions can greatly impact our personal growth and
relationships.

Supporting Each Other

Support is the pillar of strength that allows us to sail through life's
transitions with greater ease. In times of change, having a strong
support system can make all the difference in our ability to adapt
and thrive. Let's explore some ways in which we can support each
other through various major life events.

1. Career Changes

Changing careers can be a daunting process, both professionally and
emotionally. Encouraging and supporting someone through this
transition can fortify their confidence and help them pursue their
dreams. Offer to be a sounding board for their ideas, provide honest
feedback, and assist in networking opportunities. Additionally,
remind them of their strengths and the value they bring to the table,

especially during moments of self-doubt.

2. Relocation

Relocating to a new city or country can be exciting but also emotionally challenging. Help ease the transition by providing practical assistance, such as helping with packing and unpacking, assisting in finding local resources, and introducing them to new social networks. Engage in regular check-ins and be a source of emotional support, acknowledging and validating any feelings of homesickness or adjustment difficulties.

3. Marriage

Marriage is a significant life event that oftentimes requires individuals to adapt to a shared life and responsibilities. Support couples through this transition by being available to talk, offering guidance, and reminding them of the importance of open communication. Encourage them to seek premarital counseling or attend relationship workshops to equip them with essential skills for a successful partnership.

4. Starting a Family

The journey of becoming parents is transformative, both physically and emotionally. Offer support to expectant parents by helping with various tasks, like attending doctor's appointments, preparing meals, or offering to babysit older children. Be a reassuring presence during the highs and lows of pregnancy, offering a listening ear and validation of their experiences. Additionally, organize a baby shower or gather loved ones to celebrate and provide practical items for the new parents.

5. Loss of a Loved One

Experiencing the loss of a loved one can be one of the most challenging transitions in life. Offer support by being present, listening without judgment, and providing practical assistance in times of need. Encourage them to seek professional help if necessary and respect their unique grieving process. Remember that everyone mourns differently, and being patient and understanding is crucial during such times of immense emotional vulnerability.

Navigating Life Transitions: Practical Advice

While each life transition carries its own nuances, there are some general tips that can be applied across different situations. Let's explore some practical advice to help navigate major life events:

1. Embrace Change: Accept that change is a natural part of life and can often lead to personal growth and new opportunities. Embracing change with an open mind allows us to navigate transitions more smoothly.

2. Seek Support: Reach out to trusted friends, family, or professionals who can provide guidance and emotional support during times of

transition. Having a strong support network lessens the burden and helps us feel grounded.

3. Self-Care: Prioritize self-care during life transitions. Engage in activities that bring you joy and relaxation, such as exercise, meditation, or spending time in nature. Taking care of yourself equips you with the resilience needed to overcome challenges.

4. Set Realistic Expectations: Major life events often come with a myriad of expectations. It is essential to set realistic expectations for yourself and others involved. Celebrate small victories and be patient with the process.

5. Communicate Openly: Clear and honest communication is crucial during times of transition. Be open about your needs, concerns, and aspirations while also actively listening to others' perspectives. Effective communication fosters understanding and strengthens relationships.

Wrapping Up

Life transitions are inevitable, and they shape the tapestry of our lives. Embracing these transitions with empathy and support allows us to navigate through the challenges and reap the rewards that accompany change. By offering a helping hand, a listening ear, and a shoulder to lean on, we can create a nurturing and resilient environment where everyone can flourish throughout life's journey. Remember, our collective support is an invaluable gift that fuel the growth and wellbeing of those we care about.

Chapter 6: Specialized Bridge Building

In this chapter, we delve into the fascinating world of specialized bridge building. While most of us are familiar with conventional bridges that span rivers, highways, and railways, there exists a vast array of unique bridges designed for specific purposes. These specialized structures push the boundaries of engineering, showcasing remarkable innovation, and solving complex challenges. From skybridges connecting buildings and pedestrian bridges weaving through natural landscapes, to iconic architectural wonders, this chapter explores some of the most extraordinary and awe-inspiring bridges from around the world.

1. Skybridges:

Skybridges, also known as pedestrian bridges, are architectural marvels that connect buildings, allowing people to move between them at higher levels without stepping foot on the ground. These bridges not only serve as practical and convenient connectors but often become iconic landmarks themselves.

One such skybridge that captivates both locals and tourists alike is the Petronas Twin Towers Skybridge in Kuala Lumpur, Malaysia. Located on the 41st and 42nd floors of the Petronas Twin Towers, this double-decker bridge offers breathtaking views of the city. With its curved design and glass panels, it gives visitors a sense of walking among the clouds while connecting the two towers.

Another intriguing skybridge can be found in Singapore's Marina Bay Sands. This one-of-a-kind structure, called the SkyPark, is perched 200 meters above the ground, spanning across three distinct towers. The SkyPark features an infinity pool, lush gardens, and observation decks, providing visitors with a stunning panorama of the city skyline and the vast expanse of the Marina Bay.

2. Pedestrian Bridges:
Apart from connecting tall buildings, pedestrian bridges also span natural landscapes, offering leisurely pathways and enhancing the connection between communities. These bridges provide safe and convenient access while preserving the beauty of the surrounding environment.

Among the most remarkable pedestrian bridges in the world is the Golden Gate Bridge in San Francisco, California. Spanning 1.7 miles across the Golden Gate strait, this iconic bridge is an engineering marvel and a symbol of American innovation. Its distinctive orange-red color and Art Deco design have made it a beloved landmark. With designated pedestrian walkways, those on foot can enjoy stunning views of the bay while traversing the bridge.

Another noteworthy pedestrian bridge is the Millau Viaduct in southern France. Soaring over the Tarn Valley, this cable-stayed bridge holds the record for the tallest bridge in the world. With its slender piers and aerodynamic design, it seems to defy gravity. This engineering masterpiece seamlessly merges the natural beauty of the French countryside with cutting-edge technology.

3. Architectural Marvels:
Some bridges transcend mere functionality and become iconic architectural wonders. These extraordinary structures push boundaries, inspire the imagination, and capture the essence of their surroundings.

The Brooklyn Bridge in New York City exemplifies the fusion of engineering excellence and breathtaking aesthetics. When it first opened to the public in 1883, it was hailed as a wonder of the modern world. Its Gothic-inspired towers, suspension cables, and intricate details create a timeless masterpiece. Today, the Brooklyn Bridge stands as an enduring symbol of New York's industrious spirit.

In the heart of London, the Tower Bridge stands as a testament to Victorian engineering. This iconic bascule and suspension bridge, adorned with majestic towers and inspiring ornamental details, gracefully spans the River Thames. Its technical sophistication allowed it to be raised to allow tall ships to pass through, and its striking presence has made it an integral part of London's skyline.

4. Specialty and Theme-Based Bridges:

In addition to the breath-taking structures mentioned above, there exist various specialty and theme-based bridges around the world, each with its own uniqueness and charm.

For example, the Lucky Knot Bridge in Changsha, China, not only serves as a pedestrian walkway but also doubles as an art installation. Its distinctive loop-de-loop design has made it a must-see attraction, representing good luck, prosperity, and unity.
In contrast, the Ponte Vecchio in Florence, Italy, is an ancient bridge that spans the Arno River. What sets this bridge apart is the numerous shops, boutiques, and art galleries built on its sides. Dating back to the 13th century, the Ponte Vecchio conveys the rich history and vibrant culture of the city while providing a unique shopping experience.
Specialized bridge building encompasses an array of stunning structures that go beyond mere transportation. From skybridges connecting towering structures to pedestrian walkways blending seamlessly into the natural environment, and from iconic architectural wonders to specialty-themed designs, these bridges captivate our imagination, evoke emotions, and serve as integral landmarks. They illustrate the incredible capabilities of human creativity and engineering prowess. As we conclude this chapter, we are left in awe of the countless innovative bridges that continue to shape our world, both functionally and artistically.

Cross-cultural Relationship Bridges: Navigating and celebrating differences in multicultural relationships

In today's interconnected global society, multicultural relationships have become increasingly common. These relationships bring together individuals from different cultural backgrounds, providing an opportunity for shared experiences and the celebration of diverse traditions. However, they also require navigating unique challenges and building robust bridges to foster understanding, respect, and harmony. This chapter explores the dynamics of cross-cultural relationships, delving into the methods by which individuals can navigate and celebrate their differences.

Understanding Cultural Differences

Before delving into strategies for navigating cross-cultural relationships, it is essential to understand the impact of culture on individuals. Culture encompasses a range of elements, including language, beliefs, values, norms, and communication styles. These aspects influence an individual's worldview, shaping their attitudes, behaviors, and perceptions. Recognizing and appreciating these differences is the first step towards building bridges in a multicultural relationship.

Open and Honest Communication

Effective communication forms the foundation of any successful relationship, and this holds true for cross-cultural relationships as well. Encouraging open and honest communication allows individuals to express their thoughts, concerns, and emotions. It fosters an atmosphere of trust, a safe space where partners can freely discuss their cultural differences without judgment.

Active listening is a vital component of open communication. Listening attentively can help partners understand each other's perspectives, needs, and desires. Affirming the other person's feelings and experiences validates their point of view and demonstrates empathy and respect. Engaging in active listening shows a willingness to learn from and appreciate cultural disparities.

Exploration of Cultural Backgrounds

Learning about each other's cultural backgrounds is an exciting and significant part of a cross-cultural relationship. Individuals can embark on a journey of discovery by sharing their traditions, customs, festivals, and cuisine with their partners. This exchange promotes cultural appreciation and helps build a deeper connection. Celebrating significant cultural events together offers an opportunity to create new shared experiences while strengthening the bond between partners.

Incorporating Cultural Traditions

Embracing and incorporating each other's cultural traditions can be a joyful and enriching experience in cross-cultural relationships. By jointly participating in events, practices, and celebrations, partners can create a strong sense of unity and inclusion. This engagement allows each individual to showcase their cultural heritage and deepens their understanding of the significance attached to these traditions.

Flexibility and Adaptability

Flexibility and adaptability are crucial skills when entering a cross-cultural relationship. Adapting to new cultural practices, beliefs, and communication styles can be challenging, but it is a necessary step towards building bridges. Openness to change and willingness to compromise can mitigate misunderstandings and conflicts arising from cultural differences. It is essential to remember that compromise does not mean sacrificing one's own culture but finding a harmonious balance that respects both partners' backgrounds.

Navigating Language Barriers

Language barriers are a common hurdle in cross-cultural relationships. Partners may have different native languages or varying fluency in a shared language. In such cases, patience, understanding, and support are vital. Taking the initiative to learn each other's languages can foster deeper understanding and facilitate effective communication. It can also serve as a symbolic gesture of commitment to the relationship and the desire to bridge linguistic gaps.

Respecting Personal Boundaries

In any relationship, it is crucial to respect personal boundaries. Boundaries may differ based on cultural norms, and partners must be mindful of these disparities. Discussing personal boundaries openly can help set clear expectations, ensuring that both individuals feel comfortable and respected in their respective spaces.

Managing Family and Social Expectations

Cross-cultural relationships often involve managing the expectations and opinions of family and friends. Challenges can arise when individuals from different cultural backgrounds have varying perspectives on relationships. It is vital to engage in open dialogue with loved ones, explaining the significance of the relationship and seeking their understanding and acceptance. Patience, empathy, and education are key in bridging the gap between partners and their respective social circles.

Conflict Resolution

Conflict is an inevitable aspect of any relationship, but it can become more complex in cross-cultural partnerships. Cultural disparities can amplify misunderstandings and disagreements. It is crucial to approach conflicts with empathy, understanding, and a willingness to learn. Cultural differences should be viewed as an opportunity for growth rather than a source of contention. Seeking professional support, such as couples therapy, can be beneficial in navigating conflicts in a multicultural relationship.

Celebrating Individuality and Diversity

While navigating cross-cultural relationships may present unique challenges, it is essential to celebrate individuality and diversity. Embracing the richness and uniqueness of each partner's culture creates an environment of inclusivity. This celebration enhances the relationship by fostering mutual admiration, respect, and the opportunity for constant growth and learning.

Navigating and celebrating differences in cross-cultural relationships is an ongoing process requiring understanding, empathy, and dedication. This chapter has explored various strategies, ranging from open and honest communication to actively exploring cultural backgrounds and incorporating traditions. By fostering an environment of respect, patience, and learning, individuals in multicultural relationships can build strong bridges and cultivate harmonious, loving partnerships that celebrate their diverse backgrounds.

Bridging Generational Gaps: Managing and appreciating age differences in relationships

Throughout our lives, we encounter a wide range of relationships, each unique in its own way. While some relationships are formed with individuals who are similar in age and background, others bring us into close contact with individuals from different generations. These intergenerational relationships can be incredibly rewarding but can also present unique challenges. In this chapter, we will delve into the topic of managing and appreciating age differences in relationships, exploring strategies for fostering understanding, respect, and empathy across generations.

The Changing Landscape of Relationships:

In recent decades, societal norms and values have evolved significantly, leading to a shift in the dynamics of relationships. With advances in technology, globalization, and increased mobility, individuals from different generations now interact more frequently than ever before. Consequently, age gaps in relationships have become more commonplace, leading to a rich tapestry of intergenerational connections. However, these age differences are not without their challenges, often requiring individuals to navigate generational gaps in understanding, communication, and expectations.

Understanding Generational Differences:

Before diving into the intricacies of managing age differences in relationships, it is crucial to have a basic understanding of the generational cohorts. Each generation, shaped by distinct historical events and cultural influences, brings a unique set of values, beliefs, and experiences to the table.

The youngest generation, Gen Z (born between 1997 and 2012), has grown up in a world shaped by technology, social media, and globalization. They are often characterized as digital natives, with a natural inclination towards innovation and activism. On the other hand, Millennials (born between 1981 and 1996) are the bridge between traditional and modern methods, having witnessed the rise of the internet and the transformation of the workplace.

Baby Boomers (born between 1946 and 1964) experienced a period of significant social change, activism, and economic prosperity. They value hard work, loyalty, and financial stability. Finally, the Silent Generation (born between 1925 and 1945) witnessed the aftermath of World War II and the Great Depression and often uphold traditional values, family structure, and hierarchy.

Building Bridges:

Building bridges across generational gaps requires effort, empathy, and open-mindedness. Recognizing and appreciating the differences in values, beliefs, and experiences is the first step towards fostering understanding and connection. Here are a few strategies to help manage age differences effectively:

1. Active Listening: Effective communication is key to bridging the generation gap. Active listening involves paying full attention to the speaker, seeking clarification if necessary, and demonstrating empathy. By actively listening, you can gain insights into the other person's perspective and build a deeper connection.

2. Sharing Stories: Storytelling is a powerful tool that transcends generations. Sharing personal experiences, anecdotes, and stories not only provides valuable life lessons but also acts as a bridge, connecting people across different age groups. It allows individuals to understand and appreciate each other's journeys and promotes empathy.

3. Mutual Learning: An intergenerational relationship offers a unique opportunity for mutual learning. Each generation brings a distinct set of skills, knowledge, and perspectives. By embracing this

diversity, individuals can learn from one another, expanding their horizons and challenging their preconceived notions.

Navigating Challenges:

Despite the potential for growth and connection, intergenerational relationships can also present challenges. These challenges are often rooted in differences in communication styles, attitudes towards technology, and expectations of work-life balance. Here are a few strategies for navigating these challenges:

1. Open Communication: Honest and open communication is crucial when addressing potential challenges. By creating a safe space for dialogue, individuals can express their concerns, expectations, and boundaries. This allows for the establishment of clear guidelines and mutual understanding.

2. Embracing Technology: Generational gaps often manifest in differing attitudes towards technology. Younger generations tend to be more tech-savvy, while older generations may be more resistant to change. Encouraging cross-generational learning and exploration of technology can bridge this gap, enabling older individuals to feel more connected and empowered.

3. Flexibility and Adaptability: Being adaptable and open to change is essential in navigating age differences in relationships. Each generation has its own unique characteristics, strengths, and weaknesses. By remaining flexible and adjusting expectations, individuals can create a harmonious balance between generations.

Benefiting from Intergenerational Relationships:

While age differences in relationships may pose challenges, they also bring immense benefits. Intergenerational relationships offer an opportunity for personal growth, expanded perspectives, and increased mutual support. Here are a few ways individuals can benefit from these connections:

1. Mentoring and Guidance: Older individuals can serve as mentors, offering guidance, wisdom, and life lessons based on their experiences. Younger individuals, in turn, can provide fresh perspectives, technological expertise, and a willingness to challenge conventional wisdom.

2. Emotional Support: Intergenerational relationships provide a unique platform for emotional support. Different generations can offer comfort, understanding, and empathy during challenging times, based on their varied life experiences and accumulated wisdom.

3. Breaking Stereotypes: Age differences in relationships challenge stereotypes and preconceived notions about specific generations. These relationships foster understanding, debunk myths, and promote a more inclusive and accepting society.

Managing and appreciating age differences in relationships is a unique and ever-evolving journey. It requires empathy, open-mindedness, effective communication, and a willingness to learn from one another. By recognizing the generational gaps, navigating potential challenges, and embracing the benefits of intergenerational connections, individuals can create rich and meaningful relationships that transcend age boundaries.

Building through Trauma: Supporting a partner through trauma and ensuring relationship health

In any relationship, happiness and harmony can be disrupted by unforeseen events. Trauma, in particular, has the power to deeply impact an individual's mental and emotional wellbeing, which can, in turn, affect the dynamics of a relationship. However, by providing unwavering support and fostering open communication, partners can work together to build resilience and strengthen their bond. This chapter explores the importance of understanding and supporting a partner through trauma, while also ensuring the overall health and longevity of the relationship.

Section 1: Recognizing Trauma

Trauma can have various sources, such as accidents, abuse, natural disasters, or the loss of a loved one. It is vital for partners to develop an awareness of trauma's potential signs and symptoms, as they may not always be immediately apparent. Exhibiting empathy and compassion, partners can actively identify potential triggers, emotional distress, or behavioral changes. It is essential to remember that trauma affects individuals differently, so patience is key.

Section 2: Establishing a Safe Space

Trauma can lead to heightened sensitivity and fear, making it crucial to create a nurturing and safe environment within the relationship. Partners should strive to provide a judgment-free zone where open dialogue and emotional vulnerability can flourish. This safe space allows the trauma survivor to express their thoughts, fears, and concerns without the fear of rejection or criticism. Active listening and validation become invaluable tools, assuring the affected partner that their feelings are heard and respected.

Section 3: Practicing Active and Compassionate Listening

Building on the establishment of a safe space, active and compassionate listening ensures that partners feel genuinely heard and understood. It involves giving undivided attention, maintaining eye contact, and providing comforting gestures when needed. Additionally, partners should actively seek clarification when necessary to avoid misinterpreting emotions or concerns. Engaging in attentive listening allows significant progress towards healing and rebuilding trust to occur.

Section 4: Encouraging Professional Support

While partners can provide immense support, it is important to recognize the limitations of personal involvement. Trauma often requires professional assistance from therapists, counselors, or support groups experienced in trauma recovery. Encouraging and supporting the idea of seeking professional help can be a vital step towards healing and effectively managing trauma's long-term effects. By doing so, partners demonstrate their commitment to their loved one's wellbeing and reinforce the importance of expert guidance.

Section 5: Cultivating Patience and Understanding

Trauma recovery is a complex and nonlinear process, requiring patience and understanding from both partners. It is crucial to acknowledge that healing does not follow a predetermined timeline and that setbacks may occur along the way. Supporting a partner through these setbacks with empathy and grace is paramount. Partners should approach these challenges as opportunities for growth and appreciate the small victories achieved on the path to recovery.

Section 6: Building Trust

Trauma can erode an individual's ability to trust others due to a sense of betrayal or loss of control. Rebuilding trust is a gradual process that requires honesty and consistency from both partners. Trust is fostered by delivering on commitments, maintaining open lines of communication, and respecting boundaries. Partners should prioritize transparency and avoid actions that may exacerbate feelings of vulnerability or insecurity within the relationship.

Section 7: Balancing Individual Needs

While supporting a partner through trauma is essential, maintaining the overall health of the relationship requires partners to balance their individual needs. It is crucial to create space to address the well-being of each partner, fostering personal interests, friendships, and self-care. This balance allows partners to come together as individuals with unique experiences and enriching their union.

Section 8: Adapting Together

Trauma can significantly alter an individual's perspective on life and relationships. Partners must be willing to adapt their expectations and communication styles to accommodate these changes. Respecting the trauma survivor's triggers and actively working together to find coping mechanisms allows partners to grow together as they navigate the aftermath of trauma. By adapting together, the relationship can emerge even stronger and more resilient.

Section 9: Celebrating Progress and Growth

Amidst the challenges posed by trauma, partners should find opportunities to celebrate progress and growth. Recognizing and acknowledging achievements, both big and small, can reinforce the strength of the relationship and inspire further healing. Celebratory moments become an affirmation of resilience and an encouragement to continue supporting and building together.

Section 10: Hope for the Future

The journey of supporting a partner through trauma can be demanding, but it is essential to maintain hope for the future. With time, patience, and unwavering support, partners can work towards healing and rebuilding their relationship stronger than ever before. By never losing sight of the potential for growth, partners can inspire each other to find happiness, love, and fulfillment, ensuring a brighter and more resilient future together.

Supporting a partner through trauma is a challenging yet rewarding endeavor. It requires partners to be understanding, patient, and proactive in creating a safe and nurturing environment. By acknowledging the impact of trauma, fostering open communication, and encouraging professional support, partners can build a relationship that thrives even in the face of adversity. Through shared understanding and resilience, partners can emerge stronger, fostering a future filled with healing, happiness, and growth.

The Bridge of Second Chances: Insights for those in second marriages or later-life relationships

Love has no time limits. It can bloom anew at any age, bringing hope, companionship, and fulfillment. For those who find themselves in second marriages or later-life relationships, it is important to acknowledge the unique dynamics and challenges that come with starting anew. In this chapter, we will explore the intricacies of navigating a second chance at love, offering valuable insights and guidance for those embarking on this journey.

1. Reflection and Self-Awareness:

Before diving into a second marriage or later-life relationship, it is crucial to reflect on past experiences and understand the lessons learned. Take the time to analyze what went wrong in previous relationships, identifying patterns or behaviors that contributed to their demise. Self-awareness is key in order to grow, evolve, and create healthier dynamics moving forward.

Ask yourself: What personal growth have I achieved since my last relationship? What are my expectations for this new chapter in my life? By understanding your own desires, shortcomings, and emotional needs, you can better communicate your expectations with your new partner and build a foundation of trust and honesty.

2. Embrace Vulnerability:

Opening your heart to love once again can be daunting, particularly if past relationships have left you scarred or skeptical. It is normal to have reservations, but it is important not to let fear close you off from the possibilities that lie ahead. Embrace vulnerability, allowing yourself to be seen, heard, and loved by your new partner.

Remember, vulnerability is a mutual experience. Both you and your partner have likely experienced heartache and have found the strength to give love another chance. Share your stories, fears, and dreams, creating a safe space where both of you can express yourselves openly. This vulnerability will serve as the foundation for a deeply connected and nurturing relationship.

3. Blending Established Lives:

In second marriages or later-life relationships, it is common for both partners to come with established lives, including children, grandchildren, assets, and obligations. Successfully blending these separate lives can be a complex task, requiring patience and understanding from all parties involved.

Open and honest communication is paramount when navigating this aspect of your relationship. Involve your children in discussions about your new partner, ensuring their voices are heard and their concerns addressed. Make a conscious effort to blend families and create new traditions together, solidifying the bond between all family members.

4. Managing Expectations:

Each person entering a second marriage or later-life relationship brings with them a unique set of expectations and desires. To avoid disappointment and unnecessary conflict, it is crucial to manage these expectations and ensure they are realistic and attainable.

Discuss your individual expectations with your partner openly and honestly. Understand that your relationship won't be perfect, as no relationship ever is. Instead, focus on building a strong foundation of love, trust, and mutual respect. By fostering realistic expectations, you can navigate the challenges that arise with patience and grace.

5. Nurture Individual Growth:

While being in a committed relationship is a beautiful aspect of life, it is equally essential to nourish individual growth. Each person in a second or later-life relationship has their own dreams, passions, and personal development goals. Encourage and support each other's individual pursuits, allowing for personal growth to flourish within the relationship.

Take the time to explore new hobbies or interests together, or independently, fostering a sense of independence while still cherishing the togetherness you share. By nurturing individual growth, you can grow in harmony, ensuring a balanced and fulfilling partnership.

6. Embrace Change and Adaptability:

Life is ever-evolving, and so are the dynamics of second marriages or later-life relationships. Embrace change with an open mind, understanding that flexibility and adaptability are crucial for maintaining a resilient and successful union.

As you grow older together, be prepared for physical and emotional changes that come with the passage of time. Encourage open dialogue about these changes, finding ways to navigate them while still cherishing each other's evolving selves.

Continuous Learning and Growth: The importance of education and adaptability in relationships

In the journey of life, relationships play a pivotal role in our overall happiness and success. Whether it's with our partners, family, friends, or colleagues, healthy and fulfilling relationships can enrich our lives in countless ways. However, to foster and maintain such relationships, it is essential to invest in continuous learning and growth. This chapter explores the significance of education and adaptability in relationships, highlighting how they contribute to long-lasting harmony and mutual understanding among individuals.

The Evolution of Relationships:

Relationships have evolved significantly over the years, transitioning from traditional, hierarchical structures to more equitable and interdependent partnerships. In the past, relationships were often shaped by societal norms and expectations, limiting personal growth and individual freedoms. However, with changing times and progressive ideologies, relationships have become more inclusive, flexible, and based on shared values and aspirations.

Education: The Foundation of Relationship Growth:

Education, in its broadest sense, is a lifelong journey of acquiring knowledge, skills, and experiences. In the context of relationships, education serves as the foundation for personal growth and, consequently, the development of healthy connections with others. It encompasses both formal and informal learning, including academic pursuits, self-reflection, and exposure to diverse perspectives.

Formal Education:

Formal education equips individuals with the necessary intellectual tools to navigate through life, fostering critical thinking, effective communication, and problem-solving skills. It instills a sense of curiosity and a desire for continuous self-improvement, which can significantly benefit relationships. A well-educated individual can contribute to their relationships by offering valuable insights, engaging in meaningful conversations, and facilitating open-mindedness.

Informal Education:

While formal education provides structured knowledge, informal education complements it by offering experiential learning and personal growth. Informal education encompasses various avenues, such as reading books, attending workshops or seminars, participating in workshops, or engaging in hobbies that broaden one's horizons. Through continuous self-education, individuals become better equipped to understand themselves and others, fostering empathy, emotional intelligence, and adaptability.

The Role of Emotional Intelligence:

Emotional intelligence, or EQ, refers to the ability to perceive, understand, manage, and express emotions effectively. It plays a vital role in developing and maintaining healthy relationships. Education, both formal and informal, enhances emotional intelligence by cultivating self-awareness and empathy. By gaining a deeper understanding of one's emotions and those of others, individuals can navigate conflicts, communicate effectively, and build strong emotional connections.

Adaptability: The Key to Thriving Relationships:

In a constantly evolving world, adaptability is an indispensable characteristic for both individuals and relationships. Adaptability allows individuals to adjust to changing dynamics, embrace new ideas and experiences, and grow together with their partners. Relationships that lack adaptability often become stagnant or suffer from miscommunication, misunderstandings, and resentment.

Embracing Change:

Education plays a crucial role in promoting adaptability within relationships. By continuously learning and exploring new perspectives, individuals become more open to change and willing to challenge their existing beliefs and attitudes. This willingness to embrace change fosters a healthier, more dynamic relationship, where both partners support each other's growth and development.

Communication and Collaboration:

Adaptability also relates to the ability to communicate and collaborate effectively within a relationship. As individuals continuously learn and grow, their desires, needs, and perspectives may undergo transformations. In such cases, open and honest communication becomes essential to ensure mutual understanding and joint decision-making. By adapting to each other's changing circumstances, relationships can thrive and become more resilient.

Continuous Learning in Relationships:

The growth of a relationship requires a conscious commitment to continuous learning and self-improvement. This involves fostering a culture of curiosity, where both partners are encouraged to explore new interests and engage in activities that expand their knowledge and skills. By actively seeking personal growth, individuals can bring fresh perspectives and interests into their relationships, enriching the collective experiences they share.

Empowering One Another:

Education and adaptability in relationships go beyond personal growth; they also encompass empowering each other to reach their full potential. By supporting and encouraging each other's educational pursuits, partners can create an environment where both individuals feel valued and inspired. Empowerment also involves recognizing and celebrating each other's achievements, cultivating a sense of fulfillment and mutual respect.

The Impact of Education and Adaptability on Relationships:

Investing in education and adaptability strengthens relationships in numerous ways:

1. Enhanced Communication: Education equips individuals with effective communication skills, enabling them to express their thoughts and emotions openly and respectfully. Through adaptability, they learn to listen actively, understand differing viewpoints, and find common ground, fostering deeper connections.

2. Increased Empathy: Education broadens one's understanding of diverse experiences and perspectives. As individuals continuously learn and grow, they develop higher levels of empathy, allowing them to relate to others' experiences and emotions more effectively. This empathy helps build stronger bonds within relationships.

3. Problem Solving: Education and adaptability facilitate effective

problem-solving within relationships. By continuously learning, individuals gain new insights and perspectives, empowering them to approach conflicts and challenges with creativity and resilience.

4. Personal Fulfillment: Continuous learning and growth contribute to personal fulfillment within relationships. When individuals engage in educational pursuits and adapt to change, they experience a sense of accomplishment and self-actualization, positively impacting their overall well-being and, consequently, their relationships.

5. Relationship Resilience: Relationships built on education and adaptability are more resilient and better equipped to withstand the tests of time. Partners who continuously learn and grow together have a higher likelihood of weathering challenges and emerging stronger as a unit.

Continuous learning and growth are integral to building and sustaining healthy, fulfilling relationships. Education, both formal and informal, acts as a foundation for personal growth and empowers individuals to contribute actively to their relationships. By embracing adaptability, individuals foster flexibility, effective communication, and collaboration within their relationships. Education and adaptability empower individuals to navigate change, understand emotions, solve problems, and continuously evolve as individuals and partners. Embracing continuous learning and growth fosters deeper connections, emotional intelligence, and resilience within relationships to enhance overall quality of life.

Seeking External Support: When and how to engage therapists, counselors, or support groups

In this chapter, we will delve into the crucial topic of seeking external support when facing challenges or difficulties in life. Although everyone experiences ups and downs, there are times when we may require additional assistance to navigate through these tumultuous periods. Whether it is due to relationship issues, mental health concerns, or simply feeling overwhelmed by stress, therapists, counselors, and support groups can play a vital role in helping us find our way. Through this chapter, we will explore when and how to engage with these professionals and groups, empowering you to make informed decisions about your well-being.

1. Recognizing the Need for Support:

The first step to seeking external support is recognizing the need for it. Despite our best efforts, there may come a point when our coping mechanisms begin to falter, and we find ourselves struggling to cope or regain control. This can manifest in various ways, such as persistent sadness, anxiety, feeling overwhelmed, or a loss of interest in activities we once enjoyed. It is essential to pay attention to these signs and be honest with ourselves when it is becoming too much to handle alone.

2. Exploring Different Types of Support:

Once we acknowledge the need for external support, it's essential to familiarize ourselves with various options available to us. Therapists, counselors, and support groups each offer distinctive approaches to addressing our needs, and finding the right fit is crucial.

a) Therapists: Therapists are trained professionals who have expertise in helping individuals navigate their emotional and mental well-being. They provide a safe and confidential space for individuals to explore their challenges, uncover underlying issues, and develop strategies for growth and healing. Therapists employ various evidence-based therapeutic techniques, such as Cognitive Behavioral Therapy (CBT), Dialectical Behavior Therapy (DBT), and psychodynamic therapy, tailoring their approach to the unique needs of each individual.

b) Counselors: Similar to therapists, counselors offer guidance and support, primarily focusing on addressing specific issues or life challenges. They often work in educational or career-related settings, assisting individuals in making decisions, developing goals, and enhancing their overall well-being. Counselors can be particularly beneficial for those seeking help with academic, vocational, or personal development matters.

c) Support Groups: Support groups provide an invaluable resource for individuals dealing with similar issues or circumstances. These groups usually consist of individuals who have experienced or are going through similar challenges, creating a sense of understanding, empathy, and shared experiences. Support groups may be facilitated by professionals or solely peer-led. They offer a space for individuals to share their thoughts, concerns, and strategies, helping one another navigate their journeys toward healing and growth.

3. Factors to Consider when Seeking External Support:

When deciding whether to engage with a therapist, counselor, or support group, several factors need to be considered. It is important to remember that what works for one person may not necessarily work for another, so finding the right fit is crucial.

a) Personal Comfort: Feeling comfortable sharing personal thoughts and vulnerabilities is essential in any therapeutic setting. When considering external support, ask yourself whether you feel at ease with the individual or group you are considering. Trust and rapport are fundamental in establishing a productive and supportive relationship.

b) Goals and Objectives: Determine your specific goals and objectives when seeking external support. Are you looking for short-term or long-term solutions? Do you need guidance around specific challenges or a comprehensive exploration of underlying issues? Understanding your goals will help align your needs with the expertise and scope of practice of potential therapists, counselors, or support groups.

c) Accessibility and Affordability: Consider practical factors such as proximity to the support provider, appointment availability, and whether the services are covered by your insurance or fit within your budget. Accessibility and affordability can significantly impact your ability to engage consistently, which is critical for making progress.

d) Specialization and Expertise: Different support providers may have varied specializations and areas of expertise. For example, some therapists excel in treating anxiety disorders, while others may specialize in relationship counseling. Understanding the support provider's background and expertise is crucial to ensuring they can effectively address your specific needs.

4. Taking the First Steps:

Once you have identified a therapist, counselor, or support group that aligns with your needs, it is time to take the first step. Many find this initial approach intimidating, but it is essential to remember that these professionals are here to help.

a) Contacting a Therapist or Counselor: Reach out to the professional you have selected to inquire about their services. Most offer a brief consultation or phone call to discuss your needs, goals, and any concerns you may have. This initial contact will also give you an opportunity to gauge their communication style, which is key to building a productive therapeutic relationship.

b) Connecting with a Support Group: If you have chosen to engage in a support group, reach out to the facilitator or organization running the group. Inquire about the process to join and any prerequisites or expectations for participation.

Seeking external support is a brave and proactive step towards taking control of our mental and emotional well-being. By recognizing when we need help, exploring different support options, considering various factors, and taking action, we empower ourselves to navigate life's challenges with confidence and resilience. Remember, you are not alone on this journey, and seeking support is a testament to your courage and strength.

Cultivating a Shared Social Circle: The significance of mutual friends and shared social experiences

Humans are inherently social creatures, and our connections with others play a vital role in our overall well-being and satisfaction with life. While individual friendships are undoubtedly important, cultivating a shared social circle holds a unique significance. When we have mutual friends and engage in shared social experiences, we deepen our connections, enhance our social support networks, and create a sense of belonging. In this chapter, we will explore the value of cultivating a shared social circle, the benefits it brings to our lives, and how we can foster these connections to enhance our overall social experience.

The Power of Mutual Friends

Mutual friends are like a bridge that connects two individuals, creating a shared bond that goes beyond individual relationships. When we have mutual friends with someone, it not only enhances our connection with that person but also instills a sense of trust and reliability. Mutual friends serve as a testament to the people we associate with and can provide insights into their character, values, and interests.

One of the significant advantages of having mutual friends is the ability to create a support network. When faced with challenging times, having friends who know and care about both parties involved can be immensely helpful. Mutual friends can act as mediators, offering advice and perspectives from a neutral standpoint, helping to resolve conflicts, and strengthening relationships. Additionally, mutual friends can be a source of emotional support, providing reassurance, empathy, and a sense of belonging during difficult moments.

Furthermore, mutual friends can serve as a social glue, bringing people together in various social settings. Expanding our social circles through shared connections not only amplifies our opportunities for social interactions but also increases our circle of potential friends. These shared connections often lead to new and exciting experiences, creating a ripple effect that broadens our horizons and enriches our lives.

The Role of Shared Social Experiences

Shared social experiences are an integral part of our lives and can create lasting memories and connections. Whether it's attending a concert, going on a vacation, or simply gathering for a cozy dinner, these experiences allow us to connect on a deeper level and strengthen our bonds with one another.

Shared experiences carry a unique significance due to the memories and emotions attached to them. These shared memories can act as a foundation for future conversations, creating a sense of shared history and fostering a strong sense of belonging within the group. Additionally, participating in shared social experiences cultivates a sense of camaraderie, as individuals feel a shared purpose, enjoyment, or even a collective meaning in their interactions.

Moreover, shared social experiences provide a platform for personal growth and development. When we engage in new activities or adventures with others, we are exposed to different perspectives, skills, and knowledge. This exposure not only broadens our understanding of the world but also encourages personal growth, as we can learn from the experiences, opinions, and expertise of those around us.

Fostering a Shared Social Circle

Creating and cultivating a shared social circle does not happen by chance; it requires intentional efforts and active participation. Here are some strategies to help foster a shared social circle:

1. Introduce Friends: Be proactive in introducing your friends to one

another. Initiate group gatherings or events where individuals from different circles can socialize and form connections. By taking the initiative, you can help create a shared social space where mutual friendships can grow.

2. Encourage Mixers: Plan social events or activities that encourage people from different social circles to come together. This could be a themed dinner party, a sports league, or even a weekend getaway. Providing opportunities for individuals to interact and bond in a relaxed setting can bridge gaps and foster shared connections.

3. Embrace Common Interests: Identify shared interests within your social circle and build upon them. Encourage participation in activities that align with these common interests, such as joining a book club, attending art exhibitions, or exploring hiking trails. Shared interests not only strengthen existing bonds but also attract new individuals with similar affinities into your social circle.

4. Communication and Openness: Foster an environment of open communication within your social circle. Encourage individuals to express their thoughts, feelings, and needs openly. This open dialogue creates a safer and more trusting space for individuals to connect and engage with one another on a deeper level.

5. Maintain Balance: While shared social circles can be enriching, it is important to strike a balance between shared experiences and

individual friendships. Ensure that everyone has the space and freedom to nurture their individual connections while still actively participating in shared social gatherings.

Cultivating a shared social circle holds significant value in our lives. Through mutual friends and shared social experiences, we forge connections that go beyond individual relationships. The power of mutual friends lies in their ability to foster trust, reliability, and social support. Shared social experiences create lasting memories and deepen our sense of belonging within a community.

By intentionally fostering a shared social circle, we open ourselves up to new opportunities, broaden our perspectives, and enhance our overall social experience. So, let us embrace the power of cultivating a shared social circle and build deep, meaningful connections with those around us.

Regular Relationship Maintenance: Practical tips for routine check-ins and relationship tune-ups

Have you ever noticed how relationships require constant effort and nurturing to thrive? Just like a beautiful garden, they need regular maintenance to stay healthy and vibrant. In this chapter, we will explore the importance of routine check-ins and relationship tune-ups to ensure long-lasting satisfaction and growth in your relationships. Whether you are in a romantic partnership, a close friendship, or a family bond, these practical tips will guide you in making your relationships flourish.

1. Prioritize Communication:

Effective communication lays the foundation for any successful relationship. Regular check-ins provide an opportunity for open and honest dialogue. Schedule regular times to discuss each other's needs, concerns, and goals. Choose an atmosphere that is comfortable and conducive to conversation. It could be over a cup of coffee at your favorite café or during a relaxing walk in the park. Whatever the setting, ensure your check-ins are free from distractions and allow for genuine connection.

2. Practice Active Listening:

Listening is equally as important as speaking during your check-ins. Active listening involves giving your undivided attention, using non-verbal cues to show understanding, and asking clarifying questions. By truly hearing your partner's perspective, you demonstrate empathy and strengthen your bond. Remember, it's not just about hearing the words, but also understanding the emotions and intentions behind them.

3. Express Appreciation:

Regularly expressing gratitude and appreciation for your loved ones is essential for maintaining healthy relationships. During check-ins, take the time to acknowledge their contributions and efforts. Offer specific examples of why you are grateful for them, highlighting both big and small gestures. These expressions of appreciation create a positive atmosphere and reinforce their importance in your life.

4. Foster Emotional Intimacy:

Emotional intimacy forms a deep connection between individuals. During your relationship tune-ups, explore ways to deepen emotional connection with your partner. Share your thoughts, fears, achievements, and vulnerabilities. Create a space where both parties feel safe to express their true selves, knowing they will be met with compassion and support. This vulnerability and emotional intimacy will strengthen the foundation of your relationship.

5. Set Goals Together:

Individual growth is crucial, but shared goals can solidify your relationship's foundation. During check-ins, discuss and set mutual goals that align with your shared values and aspirations. These goals could be personal, professional, or relational in nature. By working towards common goals, you foster collaboration, teamwork, and a sense of shared purpose.

6. Practice Conflict Resolution:

Conflict is inevitable in any relationship. However, it is how conflicts are resolved that defines the strength of a bond. During relationship tune-ups, focus on improving your conflict resolution skills. Learn to address issues constructively, without blame or defensiveness. Use "I" statements to express how a certain behavior makes you feel, and actively listen to your partner's perspective. Seek compromise and find win-win solutions that satisfy both parties. When conflicts are resolved effectively, it enhances trust and understanding.

7. Keep the Spark Alive:

Over time, relationships can lose their initial excitement. It's crucial to prioritize maintaining the spark through small gestures and intentional efforts. Surprise your partner with gestures of love and romance. Plan unplanned dates, surprise weekend getaways, or even simple acts like leaving little love notes. Recreate the moments that made you fall in love in the first place, and allow yourselves to continually experience the joy of discovery and romance.

8. Designate Quality Time:

In today's fast-paced world, it's easy to get caught up in the busyness and neglect quality time with your loved ones. During your relationship tune-ups, make it a priority to schedule regular quality time. Put away distractions, such as phones or work-related stress, and engage in activities that promote connection and enjoyment. It could be cooking together, going for walks, watching movies, or engaging in your shared hobbies. The key is to create an environment conducive to quality bonding.

9. Support Each Other's Growth:

Throughout life, personal growth is inevitable. During check-ins, discuss your individual aspirations, dreams, and personal development goals. Encourage and support each other's growth journeys, providing space to pursue personal interests. By cherishing and supporting each other's individuality, you strengthen the relationship's foundation and foster a healthy sense of independence.

10. Adapt and Flex:

As time goes by, relationships evolve. What once worked may no longer be effective. During your relationship tune-ups, embrace a mindset of adaptability and flexibility. Be open to change and willing to adjust your approaches as needed. Recognize that both individuals are continuously growing and evolving, and be prepared to adapt accordingly. Through this adaptability, your relationship continues to evolve in a way that meets the changing needs of both parties. Maintaining healthy and fulfilling relationships requires regular check-ins and relationship tune-ups. By prioritizing communication, practicing active listening, expressing appreciation, fostering emotional intimacy, setting goals together, practicing conflict resolution, keeping the spark alive, designating quality time, supporting each other's growth, and adapting and flexing, you can ensure the long-term satisfaction and growth of your relationships. These practical tips, when implemented consistently, will nurture your relationships, unlock their full potential, and bring joy and fulfillment to both parties involved. Remember, relationships are like flowers; they require nourishment, care, and regular attention to bloom and flourish.

Chapter 7: The Bridge of Shared Experiences

The essence of any relationship lies not only in understanding each other's uniqueness but also in the shared moments that build a bridge connecting two distinct lives. This bridge, named the "Bridge of Shared Experiences," is what allows couples to traverse the vastness of their differences and come to a common space of mutual love and understanding.

1. The Foundations of the Bridge: Why Shared Experiences Matter

Shared experiences lay the foundation for trust, empathy, and deeper intimacy. Every moment a couple shares – be it laughter during a movie, the challenges faced during travel, or simply cooking a meal together – acts as a brick, strengthening the bridge between them.

2. How Shared Experiences Shape Perceptions

Over time, as couples share experiences, they build a collective memory. This memory influences perceptions and emotions. A couple might associate a certain song with their first dance or the scent of a particular perfume with a special vacation. These associations become a part of their relationship's unique narrative.

3. Bridging the Gap During Conflicts

In moments of discord, it's this bridge that can help couples reconnect. Reflecting on shared experiences can ease tension and remind couples of the love and joy they've shared, making it easier to navigate disputes and misunderstandings.

4. Creating Shared Experiences

It's essential to intentionally cultivate these moments. This might mean:

Setting aside time for regular date nights.
Traveling to new places together.
Learning a new skill or hobby as a team.
Facing and overcoming challenges together.

5. Revisiting and Celebrating Memories

Periodically reflecting on these shared memories and experiences can rekindle affection and admiration. Maybe it's watching videos from a past vacation, revisiting the restaurant from a first date, or simply reminiscing about the good times.

6. Challenges on the Bridge

Like any bridge, the Bridge of Shared Experiences can face wear and tear. It might be due to external factors like work stress, health issues, or internal factors like unresolved conflicts. It's crucial to recognize these challenges and address them head-on.

7. Repair and Maintenance

A relationship requires effort and maintenance. This means:

Actively seeking new experiences to share.
Reflecting and communicating about past experiences to understand their impact.
Engaging in couples therapy or workshops when necessary.

The Bridge of Shared Experiences is not just about the moments spent together but also the meaning derived from them. It's about how two individuals, with their unique backgrounds and perspectives, can come together to create a joint narrative. By fostering this bridge, couples can ensure that their relationship remains resilient, fulfilling, and ever-evolving.

Traveling as a Couple: The joys and challenges of exploring the world together

Traveling holds a special allure for many couples and offers a unique opportunity to strengthen their bond, create lasting memories, and foster personal growth. However, embarking on adventures as a duo, no matter how thrilling, can also present its fair share of challenges. In this chapter, we delve into the joys and challenges of traveling as a couple, offering insights, anecdotes, and practical advice to help couples make the most of their journeys together.

The Joys of Traveling as a Couple:

1. Shared Experiences: One of the most wonderful aspects of traveling as a couple is the ability to share extraordinary experiences with your beloved partner. Trekking through hidden trails, discovering breathtaking landscapes, and immersing oneself in new cultures become infinitely more meaningful when shared with a loved one. Every encounter, whether blissful or challenging, becomes a treasure to be jointly cherished for years to come.

2. Strengthened Bond: Traveling together has a unique ability to

strengthen the bond between couples. When navigating unfamiliar territories or facing unexpected situations, couples rely on each other for support, fostering a sense of unity and trust. Overcoming hurdles together creates a deep sense of shared achievement, solidifying the emotional connection and deepening the love between partners.

3. Enhanced Communication: Traveling provides an opportunity for couples to communicate and connect on a deeper level. In their day-to-day lives, couples often find themselves consumed by routines and responsibilities. However, on the road, away from the distractions of daily life, they have the chance to engage in meaningful conversations, discussing their dreams, fears, and aspirations. Traveling as a couple encourages open communication, facilitating a better understanding of each other's desires and allowing for personal growth within the relationship.

4. Memories to Last a Lifetime: The experiences shared while traveling as a couple create a treasure trove of memories that will last a lifetime. From the awe-inspiring beauty of the Eiffel Tower at sunset to the laughter-filled nights spent camping under the stars, these memories become an indelible part of the couple's journey together. Even years down the line, these memories can reignite the flame and remind them of the love and adventures they have shared.

The Challenges of Traveling as a Couple:

1. Navigating Differences: While traveling, couples may encounter differences in preferences, interests, and travel styles. One partner may be more inclined towards cultural exploration, while the other yearns for thrilling adventures. Such variations can sometimes lead to disagreements or compromises. It is essential for couples to communicate openly, respecting each other's desires and finding common ground to ensure both partners feel fulfilled during their travels.

2. Increased Intimacy and Privacy: Traveling as a couple often means sharing intimate spaces continuously, be it hotel rooms, public transport, or cramped tents. While this fosters closeness, it can also present challenges to privacy and personal space. It is crucial for couples to recognize the importance of alone time and find ways to carve out moments for themselves amidst the exhilaration of exploration.

3. Conflicting Expectations: Couples may have varying expectations regarding the purpose and outcome of their travel experiences. While one partner may prioritize relaxation and rejuvenation, the other may seek adventure and adrenaline. These discrepancies can potentially lead to disappointment or frustration. Discussing expectations and finding a middle ground before embarking on a trip can help mitigate potential conflicts, ensuring both partners have a

fulfilling experience.

4. Handling Stressful Situations: Traveling can be demanding, with unexpected obstacles and stressful situations. Lost passports, missed flights, or getting lost can test even the most harmonious relationships. It is crucial for couples to approach these challenges as a team, supporting and encouraging each other in finding solutions. Maintaining a positive outlook, retaining a sense of humor, and embracing the unpredictability of travel can help navigate these stressors and turn them into valuable life lessons.

Traveling as a couple offers a wealth of joys and challenges. It allows couples to create irreplaceable memories, deepen their bond, and foster personal growth. By acknowledging the unique dynamics of traveling as a couple and embracing open communication, mutual respect, and compromise, couples can transform their adventures into transformative experiences that will leave an indelible mark on their relationship and individual lives. So, pack your bags, hold your partner's hand, and embark on a journey of a lifetime, as the world awaits your love story.

Nurturing Shared Hobbies: Cultivating mutual interests for deeper connection

In the vast realm of human relationships, few things bring people closer together than sharing common interests and hobbies. It is through engaging in activities that resonate with both individuals that a deeper connection can be fostered. Shared hobbies not only provide an avenue for quality time spent together but also offer an opportunity for personal growth and exploration. In this chapter, we will delve into the significance of nurturing shared hobbies and discover how cultivating mutual interests can strengthen and enrich our relationships.

The Importance of Shared Hobbies:

Shared hobbies act as a bridge that connects individuals on a deeper level. When we participate in activities that speak to our passions, it allows us to bring our whole selves into the relationship. Whether it be a love for art, literature, music, or outdoor adventures, finding common ground with our loved ones creates a sense of camaraderie, understanding, and shared experiences. In fact, psychologists suggest that couples who have shared hobbies report higher levels of satisfaction and overall relationship quality.

Building Stronger Bonds:

Engaging in shared hobbies not only solidifies the bond between individuals but also fosters a closer emotional connection. When we immerse ourselves in activities that we both enjoy, we create a safe space for vulnerability and openness. Sharing our passions and creative endeavors allows us to understand one another's perspectives, hopes, and dreams, ultimately building trust and intimacy. This deeper connection can extend beyond romantic relationships to friendships and family dynamics, enriching every aspect of our lives.

Discovering Common Interests:

The journey towards nurturing shared hobbies first begins with the exploration of one another's interests. Take the time to ask your partner, friend, or family member about their hobbies, passions, and dreams. Engage in conversations that invite them to share and express themselves without judgment. Likewise, be open and transparent about your own interests. By fostering an environment of curiosity and exploration, you can uncover common ground that serves as the foundation for cultivating mutual interests.

Creating a Shared Hobby Toolbox:

Once you have discovered shared interests, it is essential to create a toolbox of activities and hobbies that both individuals can explore together. This toolbox serves as a wellspring of ideas that can be revisited and expanded upon over time, ensuring a sustained connection and continuous growth. It can include activities such as cooking classes, hiking trips, painting sessions, or book clubs. Remember, the key is to choose activities that resonate with both parties and are flexible enough to adapt with evolving interests.

Embracing New Experiences:

As you embark on this journey of nurturing shared hobbies, it is crucial to embrace new experiences and step out of your comfort zones. Trying something new together not only adds excitement and novelty to the relationship but also cultivates personal growth. Encourage each other to explore activities that one might have never considered before, allowing for self-discovery and expanding horizons. Remember, mutual interests can be fluid and ever-changing, so remain adaptive and open to new possibilities.

Fostering Collaboration:

Shared hobbies often involve collaborative efforts, which in turn foster teamwork and compromise. Whether it be a joint DIY project, creating a piece of artwork together, or planning an event, collaboration brings people closer as they work towards a common goal. Through collaboration, individuals in a relationship learn valuable skills such as effective communication, problem-solving, and negotiation. These newfound abilities extend beyond the shared hobbies and become invaluable tools for navigating other aspects of the relationship as well.

Balancing Solo Pursuits:

While cultivating mutual interests is essential for nurturing a deeper connection, it is equally vital to respect and encourage solo pursuits. Each individual in a relationship brings with them a unique set of passions and hobbies that might not necessarily align with the other person's interests. Recognize the importance of maintaining individual identities and personal growth. Encouraging and supporting each other's solo pursuits not only strengthens the bond but also encourages independence and self-discovery, which are essential pillars for a healthy relationship.

Time Management and Prioritization:

In the midst of our fast-paced lives, it is crucial to prioritize spending quality time engaging in shared hobbies. Make a conscious effort to carve out regular moments dedicated to nurturing the mutual interests that bring you closer together. This may require careful time management and prioritization of activities that truly matter. By placing importance on shared hobbies, you demonstrate commitment and dedication to the relationship, ultimately reaping the rewards of a stronger bond and enhanced connection.

Nurturing shared hobbies is a transformative journey that leads to a deeper connection, increased satisfaction, and personal growth within relationships. By exploring each other's interests, creating a shared hobby toolbox, embracing new experiences, fostering collaboration, and balancing solo pursuits, we can cultivate mutual interests that stand the test of time.

The bonds forged through shared hobbies become lasting pillars of connection, reminding us that the beauty of relationships lies in the shared experiences and growth that transcend the boundaries of individuality.

Bridging Moments of Joy: Celebrating milestones, achievements, and everyday happiness together

Life is a roller coaster ride filled with ups and downs, challenges, and hurdles. During our journey, we come across various milestones, achieve significant accomplishments, and experience little moments of joy that contribute to our overall happiness. These moments may seem fleeting, but they have the potential to bring immense happiness and strengthen our relationships.

In this chapter, we will explore the importance of celebrating milestones, achievements, and everyday happiness together. We will delve into the ways these celebrations bridge gaps in relationships, create lasting memories, and foster a sense of camaraderie. By acknowledging the impact of these moments on our lives, we can enhance our connections with loved ones and deepen our overall happiness.

Section 1: The Significance of Celebrating Milestones

1.1: Acknowledging Personal Growth

Milestones mark significant periods in our lives and symbolize personal growth and progress. From graduating college to landing a dream job or purchasing a first home, these milestones provide a sense of accomplishment and pride. By celebrating these achievements, we acknowledge the effort, dedication, and perseverance it took to reach such significant stages.

1.2: Strengthening Bonds

Celebrating milestones not only acknowledges personal growth but also strengthens the bonds between individuals. When loved ones come together to commemorate achievements, it fosters a supportive environment filled with love and encouragement. It allows us to share our joy with others, creating lasting memories and deepening our connections.

Section 2: The Power of Acknowledging Achievements

2.1: Boosting Confidence and Motivation

Recognizing achievements, no matter how big or small, is crucial as it boosts one's confidence and motivates us to strive for further success. Encouragement and celebration from friends, family, or colleagues provide a strong foundation for personal and professional growth. Celebrating achievements together creates an environment that nurtures positivity, perseverance, and a sense of self-belief.

2.2: Cultivating a Sense of Gratitude

Acknowledging achievements not only boosts confidence but also cultivates gratitude. By celebrating achievements and sharing our successes with others, we develop a sense of appreciation for the support and opportunities that led to those achievements. Gratitude allows us to acknowledge the contribution of others and creates a cycle of kindness and support within our relationships.

Section 3: Embracing Everyday Happiness

3.1: Finding Delight in the Small Things

While milestones and achievements provide significant moments of joy, everyday happiness is equally important. Embracing the beauty of small things - a warm cup of coffee in the morning, a heartfelt conversation with a friend, or a beautiful sunset - can bring spontaneous joy into our lives. By sharing these moments of everyday happiness with loved ones, we create an atmosphere where joy is contagious, fostering positivity and contentment.

3.2: Strengthening Relationships through Shared Happiness

Whether it's celebrating the completion of a personal project or savoring a delicious meal, sharing moments of everyday happiness with others creates a sense of togetherness. These shared experiences strengthen relationships, deepen connections, and remind us of the joy that lies in simple moments. By cherishing and celebrating everyday happiness together, we infuse our relationships with positivity and create a support system that enriches our lives.

Section 4: Nurturing Relationships through Celebration

4.1: Creating Lasting Memories

Celebrating milestones, achievements, and everyday happiness creates lasting memories that we can reflect upon in the future. These memories provide a sense of nostalgia, reminding us of our growth, accomplishments, and the meaningful connections we have forged. By commemorating and cherishing these moments together, we create a tapestry of shared experiences that strengthen the bonds between individuals.

4.2: Mend Gaps and Unite Diverse Perspectives

Celebrations have the power to bridge gaps and bring people with different perspectives together. By acknowledging and appreciating one another's milestones and achievements, we develop empathy, understanding, and respect for each other's journeys. These celebrations enable us to transcend differences and create a sense of unity, fostering an atmosphere of inclusivity, and love.

In this chapter, we have explored the significance of celebrating milestones, achievements, and everyday happiness together. From acknowledging personal growth to boosting confidence, embracing everyday joy, and nurturing relationships, celebrations hold the power to bridge gaps, create lasting memories, and foster a sense of camaraderie.

By recognizing the importance of these celebrations, we can enhance our relationships and our overall happiness. Together, let us embark on a journey to cherish and celebrate life's milestones, achievements, and everyday happiness, as we build a support network filled with love, encouragement, and appreciation for one another.